LIVERPOOL
ONE

The Zig Zag stair which provides a key route from Paradise Street to the higher level cinema, restaurants and park. The design team had to deal with an 11-metre fall in the site's topography.

LIVERPOOL
ONE REMAKING A CITY CENTRE

David Littlefield

A John Wiley and Sons, Ltd, Publication

Executive Commissioning Editor: Helen Castle
Project Editor: Miriam Swift
Publishing Assistant: Calver Lezama

ISBN 978-0-470-71409-6 (H/B)

Cover and book design by Nik Browning
Cover and book production by Kate Ward
Principal photography by Paul McMullin

Printed and bound in Italy by Conti Tipocolor
Last reprint September 2009

This book has been published with the support of Grosvenor

GROSVENOR

CONTENTS

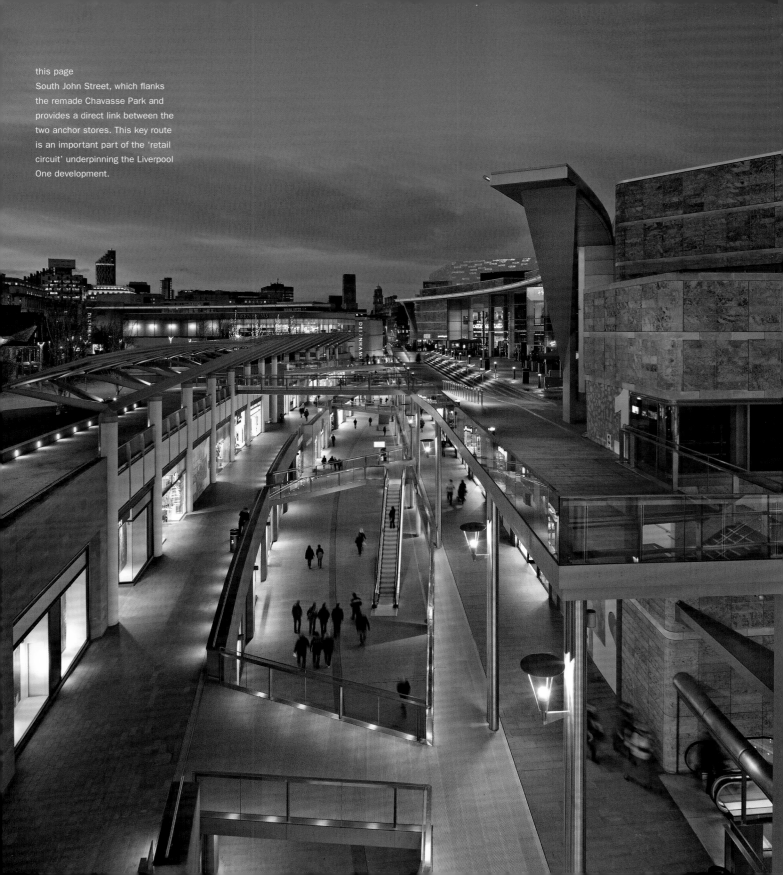

this page
South John Street, which flanks
the remade Chavasse Park and
provides a direct link between the
two anchor stores. This key route
is an important part of the 'retail
circuit' underpinning the Liverpool
One development.

LIVERPOOL ONE

Foreword by The Duke Of Westminster

For more than three centuries Grosvenor has built places where people want to live, work and spend leisure time. The property business should be as much about people as it is about buildings, streets and squares; it should be concerned with making cities vibrant both by day and by night.

You cannot give up on a substantial and historically important city like Liverpool; Grosvenor recognised that the right kind of retail-led regeneration would help to transform the city. We wanted to create a place at the heart of Liverpool that people would enjoy rather than suffer. It would have been easier to have built a rather soulless shopping centre but that would have been the wrong approach for one of the world's best known cities. Others will come to judge whether we have succeeded in our endeavour, but I am proud we delivered on our promises and did not take the easy route. Liverpool One is a celebration of how contemporary architecture and urban design can be dignified, uplifting and relevant to the way people want to use modern cities.

Liverpool One was an ambitious undertaking. Because we live in the 21st century, this project was unlike the London estates which the Grosvenor family built in the 18th and 19th centuries: this was a complex, brownfield, inner-city site that demanded enormous amounts of public consultation and approval. The desire to create a place of delight and generosity of vision is the same as it always was, but the conditions in which we work are now rather different. We had to negotiate our way through two public inquiries and satisfy policy at local and national level without allowing our vision to become stifled or diluted by bureaucracy. That requires skill, diplomacy, leadership and self-belief.

Liverpool One is a demonstration of what can be achieved when working in a spirit of true partnership with local people and their representatives. Opening the new city centre park on 1 October 2008 was one of the proudest moments of my life. I am also proud of the 5,000 full-time jobs that have been created as a direct consequence of Liverpool One, quite apart from the 3,000 jobs that went with its construction.

Grosvenor is determined to build and manage places for the betterment of people's lives. Liverpool, once the second city of the British Empire, was a powerful maritime commercial hub whose influence ebbed away as the ships went elsewhere. There has always been, however, something special about this city; Liverpool had to renew itself and face the future afresh at some point. That time is now. It is immensely satisfying that, with Liverpool One, Grosvenor has played such a key role in that resurgence.

Chapter 1
HISTORICAL CONTEXT

Chapter 1
HISTORICAL CONTEXT

Origins and growth

The evolution of a city is so slow, complex and political that it is not always possible to pin massive and irreversible change to specific dates. Events in the lives of cities are rarely so self-contained that historians can mark on a calendar when something occurred that was complete and profound enough to change things for ever. The 7 and 8 May 1941 are rare exceptions to that rule in the history of Liverpool, when the city's centre was almost entirely obliterated in a series of air raids; since then the life of Liverpool has rarely been punctuated by events of such potency and specificity. *Perhaps* the fracas on 3 July 1981 which led to the Toxteth riots (prompting Michael Heseltine, a prominent member of the then government, to examine inner-city deprivation) is an event to conjure with. 'Alone, every night ... I would stand with a glass of wine, looking out at the magnificent view over the river, and ask myself what had gone wrong for this great English city', Heseltine later told *The Guardian* newspaper.

The more recent history of Liverpool may hinge on a more commonplace event, on 5 June 1999, when the city council placed an advertisement in the *Financial Times* and the *Estates Gazette* asking for expressions of interest in the comprehensive regeneration of a run-down slice of the city centre known as the Paradise Street Development Area (often called the Bluecoat Triangle). The consequences were extraordinary. The posting of this advertisement, a decade in the making, led directly to the appointment of Grosvenor to rebuild the centre of Liverpool. This £1 billion project,

below

Liverpool in 1680. The enclosed
wet dock, on which the city's wealth
was founded, is yet to be built.
Derby Square, which is adjacent
to Grosvenor's Liverpool One
development, now occupies the
site of the castle, seen on the right
of the picture. Artist unknown.

THE SOUTH WEST PROSPECT OF LIVERPOOLE, IN THE COUNTY PALATINE OF LANCASTER

'The South West Prospect of Liverpoole, in the County Palatine of Lancaster.' Engraving by Samuel Buck and Nathaniel Buck, 1728, incorporating the newly-constructed enclosed dock (right of picture's centre). The dock was to be filled in a century later, creating Canning Place – the location of Liverpool One's new bus station.

A view of Liverpool from Seacombe, 1815, by John Jenkinson. By now Liverpool is a thriving port.

which came to fruition during 2008, is a key component of a wider ambition to put Liverpool back in the league of prominent, first rate European cities. What is significant about Liverpool One, as the Paradise Project has come to be known, is that it is the first major development to be driven by all the hard thinking on urban design and city living that went on in the 1990s. Moreover, this project also demonstrates that the 'urban renaissance' agenda – a raft of Labour government-sponsored initiatives aimed at reinvigorating the UK's town centres – actually works in practice. Grosvenor, with Liverpool City Council and the myriad other agencies and interested parties that have been scooped up by the gravity of the project, have delivered a new urban district that integrates seamlessly with the rest of the city (rather than turning its back on it), while being lively, well designed, accessible and of appropriate scale; it is also immensely popular, unique and entirely contextual. And it is big: at 42 acres, Liverpool One was the largest inner city development anywhere in Europe for many years.

During the 19th century, Liverpool rose to world dominance and trade continued to increase in spite of the abolition of slavery in 1807

The city of Liverpool marks its beginnings in 1207 when King John, in order to establish a jumping off point to Ireland, granted city status to a tiny settlement beside a muddy creek, the original 'pool' which was an offshoot of the vast River Mersey. Little changed in this sleepy backwater for the next 400 years, but by the 17th century the forces of history had started to work on it – trade with the Americas, including the lucrative trafficking of slaves, began to change the fortunes of Liverpool. The city was also given an unexpected boost when London merchants relocated there from the capital after the catastrophic Great Fire of 1666. The city owes its greatness, however, to the 18th century, a period which witnessed the city's population grow from around 5,700 to 78,000. The key to this growth was the construction of the world's first commercial 'wet dock', a gated enclosure into which ships could sail at high tide and lie protected from the winds and strong currents of the river. This dock, built over the creek that made Liverpool commercially interesting in the first place, opened in 1715 and catalysed the construction of all the other docks that now flank the city's south-western shore. In fact, the sheltered position of that original structure (built for £6,000) contained within it the seed of its own demise; all subsequent docks were built outwards into the river, expanding the mass of the emerging city by pushing into the water. The original refuge, therefore, became isolated from the Mersey and its waters became limpid and filthy. Moreover, this dock pushed right into the heart of the emerging city, taking up space that might more usefully be built upon. Why retain an inland pool when larger facilities could be constructed directly onto the river? A little over a century after its construction, in 1827, the pool that set Liverpool on the

path to becoming a maritime centre was filled in to create Canning Place, upon which was built a domed Custom House designed in the classical style. This building would surely have become one of Liverpool's landmarks had its burned out hulk been refitted after the Second World War rather than expensively demolished.

The ghosts of both wet dock and Custom House still remain present in the urban grain of the city, however. The presence of the dock forced a rectangle of streets to be wrapped around it, and this grid was preserved when Canning Place was built atop it. Even today, in spite of the hotchpotch of postwar rebuilding and neglect, the form of this rectangle can still be picked out within the Liverpool One masterplan. Indeed, beside a new department store a pavement window allows passers-by to peer into the depths of the city's archaeology.

During the 19th century, Liverpool rose to world dominance, and trade continued to increase in spite of the abolition of slavery in 1807. The massive expansion of its dock infrastructure, built to accommodate ever larger ships, made the city far and away the UK's most important port. By 1901 its population had risen to 685,000, and was expanding by about 10,000 people a year, while the docks were handling up to 11,000 ships annually. Although the number of vessels coming and going remained roughly the same in 1900 as in the 1830s, the amount of tonnage passing through Liverpool increased 10 times over the same period due to the size of the ships the city could

handle. The Port of London was, in fact, dealing with larger numbers of ships, but Liverpool was processing far greater tonnage than the capital. A century ago, more than one fifth of Britain's mighty merchant navy was registered in Liverpool. By the 1920s, the city's dockside had long ceased to be the misty, gas-lit vista of masts and horsedrawn carriages painted so romantically by John Atkinson Grimshaw. 'Yellow water, bellowing steam ferries, white trans-Atlantic liners, towers, cranes, stevedores, skiffs, shipyards, trains, smoke, chaos, hooting, ringing, hammering, puffing, the ruptured bellies of the ships, the stench of horses, the sweat, urine, and waste from all the continents of the world ... and if I heaped up words for another half an hour, I wouldn't achieve the full number, confusion and expanse which is called Liverpool,' wrote Czech writer Karel Čapek, who visited the city in 1924.

The wealth generated by this activity resulted in the creation of not just the very functional and muscular docking complexes, but also in buildings and infrastructural works of great daring and ambition. An integrated sewer system was built before London embarked on its own clean-up programme and civic buildings of considerable grandeur were erected – notably (apart from the Custom House) St George's Hall and the Edwardian trio which have given Liverpool its distinctive brand, the 'Three Graces' (the Mersey Docks and Harbour Board; the Royal Liver Building; and the Cunard Building). There are also some surprises, including Oriel Chambers and 16 Cook Street, both constructed by local builder Peter Ellis in the 1860s, which are so astonishingly before their time with all their glazing, modularity and vertical emphasis that it is a wonder they aren't more widely known. The engineering achievement of the docks themselves was also impressive and highly influential; a photograph of the gate at Gladstone Dock found itself on the pages of

this page
Launch of the Mauretania II at
Cammell Laird shipyard, across
the Mersey at Birkenhead, 1938.

right
The Georges Dock ventilation
building and Liverpool Overhead
Railway, 1936. The railway, known
as the 'dockers' umbrella', was
demolished in 1957.

Le Corbusier's 1923 classic *Towards a New Architecture* as an example of technical achievement and the aesthetic of the times.

Early in the 20th century, Liverpool also embarked on a pair of giant ecclesiastical projects, both of which sit on elevated land away from the waterfront. Only Giles Gilbert Scott's immense and powerful Anglican Cathedral was finished, while Edwin Lutyens's more ambitious design for a domed Catholic equivalent got only as far as the crypt. The building, begun in the 1930s, was completed to a different design by Sir Frederick Gibberd in 1967. Circular and unquestionably distinctive, it is nevertheless not universally popular. Liverpool architect and academic Brian Hatton damns it as a 'substitute wigwam – cheap, crude and corny'.

Decline

The harsh tone of that critique can be applied to much of Liverpool's postwar history. The bombs that fell in 1941 appear to have unleashed decades of civic incompetence, in-fighting and a lowering of ambition that had no precedent in the history of the city. The postwar period saw Liverpool fall into steep decline – the population literally halved from its 1930s' peak of 900,000 and the Albert Dock, which lies at the heart of the city's 8 mile-long strip of anchorages, closed in 1972 because it wasn't equipped to handle the large container vessels which came to characterise modern shipping. Liverpool's economy was so closely bound up with the fortunes of its waterfront that the end of the British Empire and increased competition from emerging harbours put the city on the back foot. The raw capitalism on which the city had been founded simply refocused its attentions, taking with it the entrepreneurialism, jobs and wealth that had made Liverpool a force to be reckoned with. Liverpool had even had its own clearing bank, Martins, which was subsumed by Barclays in 1971, while a series of new towns extracted people, energy and resources from what had been the regional powerhouse. British manufacturing, including shipbuilding, had long been in decline but the malaise hit Liverpool particularly hard. Such was the depth of the decline that in 1994 the city received the mixed blessing of being a recipient of Objective One funding, a programme set up to aid the European Union's poorest regions (the Highlands and Islands of Scotland received similar help at the same time). It was a mixed blessing because, although a lot of money was at stake, it was frankly embarrassing that this once great city actually qualified for it. Jack Stopforth, chief executive of Liverpool's Chamber of Commerce, is sanguine about this development, however: 'The point of Objective One funding is to enable cities to come to terms with structural change. Cities all over the world that based their livelihood on their ports have had to come to terms with change'.

right
A view across Liverpool towards the emerging Anglican Cathedral, under construction in 1934.

Liverpool One Remaking a city centre

Brian Hatton, quoted above, notes in the *Architectural Review* that Liverpool's fall from grace should not be laid squarely at the door of fickle capitalism. Part of the problem, he argues, is London's dominance of the UK and the fact that wealth and egos have long been drawn to the capital, siphoning off to the South-East the spoils of trade that were won in the North-West. So Liverpool's Sir Henry Tate, the sugar baron, found himself endowing an art gallery in London rather than one in Liverpool; similarly, Sir Thomas Beecham (of Beecham's Powders) used the wealth gained from his family's St Helens pharmaceutical concern to establish an orchestra in London, while another local chemical magnate, Dr Ludwig Mond, donated his cache of paintings to the National Gallery. If the UK's system of government was configured more along the lines of powerful, regional statelets, such as those in Germany, Liverpool might have managed to do more than merely cling on.

In the middle of Liverpool's decline, and perhaps even accelerating it, trade unionism and the Militant Tendency (a far-left faction of the Labour Party) took a firm grip on the city, and in the 1980s Liverpool came to be closely identified with restrictive practices and political confrontation. Very public rows between both Militant and Labour, and Militant and Margaret Thatcher's Conservatives, took place against a backdrop of physical urban decay. The many attempts at rebuilding were often well intentioned but naïve miscalculation at best, or plain cynicism at worst. In the late 1960s the bomb-damaged zone immediately adjacent to the Albert Dock was partially 'redeveloped' with the construction of a multistorey car park, a bus station and a bunker-like hotel, while remaining areas were grassed over as 'parkland'. The character of the area can be seen in maps from the 1980s which illustrate the plentiful supply of small, surface-level car parks. What had once been a grand boulevard comprising North and South Castle Streets, with the dome of the Town Hall at one end and the even larger dome of the Custom House at the other, had vanished. 'South Castle Street and Canning Place were not just flattened; they were erased from the map. Sailmakers' Row, the Sailors' Home, and the Piranesian Duke's Warehouse went to be replaced by car parks; while an act of civic vandalism replaced the Cotton Exchange's grandiloquent hall and Neo-Baroque front by the coarsest grade of commercial block,' writes Brian Hatton. That wasn't all. The elevated railway (the 'dockers' umbrella') that had opened in 1893 and ran the length of the city's port infrastructure, was closed and dismantled in 1957. The Albert Dock itself narrowly escaped demolition in the 1970s after it was upstaged by the new container terminal towards the mouth of the Mersey estuary at Bootle; the entire South Docks complex, which was later to gain

Frameworks and guidelines

In May 1999 Liverpool City Council issued a *Planning Framework* for the Paradise Street Development Area. Particular requirements included:

- delivering a retail development providing approximately 1 million square feet (93,000 square metres) of modern and functional retail space, including at least two new department stores;
- ensuring the development contains a mix of uses;
- incorporating sustainable development principles, including public transport accessibility;
- providing a safe and attractive environment, of high quality materials;
- providing pedestrian links to surrounding areas;
- ensuring the development enhances its surrounding area;
- ensuring provision of road links and high quality car parking.

An *Urban Design Study*, establishing guidelines for the PSDA, was published by Liverpool City Council in October 1999. Its principal recommendations included:

- retaining listed buildings and other buildings of interest and character;
- retaining at least some of the pre-existing street pattern;
- maximising 'permeability' (that is, through routes, eliminating dead-ends) over a 24-hour period;
- reinforcing the character of the city centre, especially the physical and commercial link with the sea;
- responding to the 'scale and massing' of buildings and the 'metropolitan character' of Liverpool;
- exploiting the changes in level across the site (there is a 36 foot (11 metre) fall, reflecting the route of the original inlet around which Liverpool was built);
- creating 'active perimeter frontages', such as shop fronts rather than blank walls;
- providing full access from the main shopping route of Church Street;
- relocating any business or activity that is inappropriate for the redeveloped site;
- creating high quality, open, public space;
- creating links to neighbouring districts, such as the Rope Walks, the central business district and the waterfront.

The Paradise Street Development Brief, essentially the guidelines for the prospective developer of the site, was drawn up for the city council by planning consultants Healey & Baker and issued in November 2000. This important document embraced and developed the points outlined above, including:

- developing a high quality scheme adjacent to an area which would probably be designated a World Heritage Site;
- providing spaces for quality department stores and a range of other large stores;
- providing retail units of sufficient size and quality to attract retailers not present in Liverpool, including specialist retailers;
- encouraging the use of public transport and providing convenient bus facilities;
- creating public spaces and facilities other than retail to enhance the city centre for residents and tourists, and to improve city centre 'vitality and viability' after normal shopping hours.

protected status as a conservation area, was allowed to silt up. Liverpool was in danger of being left with a world class architectural heritage, but little else.

Architectural practice Building Design Partnership (BDP) described the Rope Walks district around Duke Street, a once thriving city centre neighbourhood close to the waterfront, as suffering from 'a legacy of dereliction and decay' in a report written in 1998. 'The early development of the area is demonstrated by the tall warehouses, which form one of the most important surviving groups of their type in the country. These developed as a result of the need to derive as much commercial space as possible close to the port … As the port activities declined so too did Duke Street and its environs. This economic decline is only too well demonstrated by the deterioration of the physical fabric. The opportunity to move elsewhere and build new premises to required specifications has meant many of the buildings in the area have lain unoccupied for many years.' Of all the buildings in the area, around a quarter were vacant and a good many of them were either in poor condition or derelict. Michael Burchnall, a senior planning figure at Liverpool City Council, made similar observations of the nearby 'Bluecoat Triangle', the district surrounding the historic Bluecoat Arts Centre which now sits adjacent to Liverpool One. '[It] has persisted in its present poor state, characterised by under-used, empty and dilapidated premises, for in excess of 40 years,' he reported to a planning inquiry in 2003.

Unfortunately, the real sadness of this lament is the list of projects that were either not completed or failed to deliver on the original vision. Lutyens's cathedral project has already been mentioned, but a more damning example of failure is the Liverpool Garden Festival initiative of 1984. The festival was kick-started by the Conservative government via the Merseyside Development Corporation, a centrally appointed body which had been granted planning powers (in lieu of the city council) over a swathe of central Liverpool a few years earlier. The idea was to demonstrate that, in an area not far from where the Toxteth riots had taken place, a run-down slice of post-industrial scrub could be

reinvented as prime real estate. 'In 1981 the site of the festival was nothing but wasteland,' runs the commentary over a short promotional film of the festival. 'Derelict land was covered with rubbish tips. There were ... miles of flat, abandoned landscape.' The festival itself was, indeed, a success; but having made a former Merseyside dock presentable, most of the land has lain fallow ever since the festival closed in October 1984. Housing has been constructed on part of the site, but the rest has become embarrassingly overgrown and careworn – a rubbish tip once more. The radical city administration of the 1980s was more interested in the social issues of outlying areas and chose not to participate in Thatcher-led city centre regeneration.

Almost two decades later Everton Football Club began to hatch serious plans to relocate its stadium and build a larger, 55,000-seat facility on Liverpool's Kings Dock, another (more central) element within the city's South Docks complex. However, financing difficulties caused the project to be brought to a halt in 2003. Liverpool was, in the words of a writer for the *Liverpool Daily Post*, 'a city on the verge of falling over the edge'. The Kings Dock has since become, in fact, the site for a rather successful arena and convention centre.

More embarrassing than the stadium bid, however, was the collapse of the 'Fourth Grace' project, a colourful and daring architectural escapade combining residential, commercial and cultural spaces. Conceived to provide Liverpool with an icon that would bring the city back to global attention, the design competition ended with a shortlist comprising four of the UK's strongest architects: Richard Rogers, Norman Foster, Ted Cullinan and Will Alsop. 'We want the Fourth Grace to be a statement of intent – that Liverpool is a world-class city with world-class architecture fitting for the 21st century,' said Councillor Mike Storey, then leader of Liverpool City Council. Alsop's scheme won the competition but his 'Cloud' proposal quickly ran into difficulties, mainly over financing and the lack of a specific brief. A number of apartments were included within the design, but changing

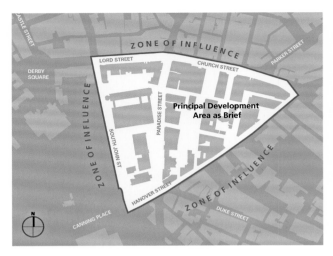

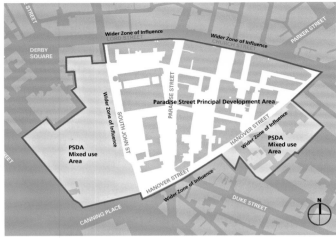

conditions meant the whole project needed to become almost overwhelmingly residential to make the figures stack up. The danger was that the Fourth Grace would become a residential project which all but smothered a publicly sponsored cultural facility. A large number of redesigns of the scheme failed to convince the project's main public sponsors and the building was cancelled in July 2004. What made this decision particularly tricky was that Alsop's design had featured prominently in Liverpool's successful bid to become the European Capital of Culture in 2008, and some from the other 11 rival cities felt that Liverpool had won the bid under false pretences. To make matters worse for the city, a highly developed scheme to reintroduce trams to Liverpool was cancelled in November 2005 after the national government refused to increase its funding package to take account of price rises. Peter Millea, a city councillor with particular responsibility for regeneration, called the decision a 'kick in the teeth for the people of Liverpool'.

One could be forgiven for thinking that conditions in Liverpool have made it difficult, if not impossible, to deliver anything like a major project. Worse than that, it would appear that Liverpool's rival further east, Manchester, was more adept at steering itself through big development projects – certainly, the manner in which the city built its way out of the aftermath of a powerful IRA bomb explosion in 1996 was impressive. Furthermore, Manchester had a fight on its hands with the Trafford Centre, a large out-of-town shopping complex which opened in 1998 after more than a decade of difficult planning inquiries; the retail competition presented by this large new mall forced Manchester's authorities to act quickly and demonstrate strong leadership. Liverpool's problems were less direct, however – more a long-term malaise than a sudden shock, to which responses are more obvious. The city, however, has never quite given up on itself and there might well be some truth behind the myth of the indomitable Scouser – proud, cheeky, resilient and apt to bounce back from setbacks more determined than ever.

The Paradise Street Development Area

Even a very quick look at a map of Liverpool will indicate the importance of the area now occupied by Liverpool One. Located on the historic centre of the city, where the very first wet dock had been constructed, this 42 acre site links the waterfront to everything beyond. Its early importance, long before the city exploded into a modern metropolis, is revealed by the number of streets that spin out from (and serve) it. In the mid 18th century Duke Street, Hanover Street, Castle Street and Paradise Street all converged on this central zone, and they still do. Comprehensively bombed in

1941 (Liverpool was the UK's second most bombed city after London), the flattened site became nothing but an interruption between the city itself and the historic docks to the south: Canning, Salthouse and Albert. Plans for the redevelopment of this area can be traced back as far as 1958 and even the sporadic developments of the late 1960s, since regretted and largely now demolished, were actually inspired by a 'city centre plan' which incorporated the 'Strand/Paradise Street Comprehensive Development Area'. The rescue and rehabilitation of this zone were important for two principal reasons. First, to link the city back to its waterfront, which had thankfully been designated a conservation area in 1976. Second, to expand Liverpool's shopping district and regain the city's status as the pre-eminent regional retail destination – even the much smaller and more provincial Chester was beginning to provide an attractive alternative to shopping in Liverpool.

right
In this drawing, the centrality of the Paradise Street area is emphasised. Occupying the space between the main shopping streets, the commercial district, the cathedrals and docks, the regeneration of the city centre had to strengthen links across Liverpool – and create them where there were none.

below
The lives of Liverpool through mapping. The original creek and early street pattern of the city are shown in white; the expanded city, including the waterfront developments which push out into the Mersey, are indicated in pale blue; the periphery of the Paradise Street Development Area, now known as Liverpool One, is picked out in orange. Paradise Street follows the line of the creek, while the ground rises to its west forming a promontory where a castle was once located.

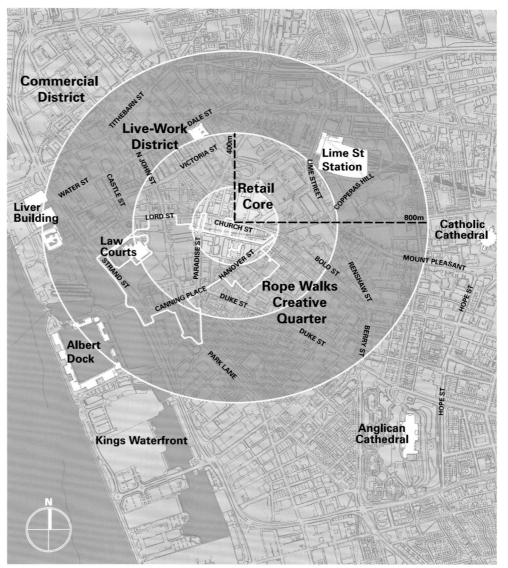

Although the Albert Dock was given Grade 1 protection in 1952, this important listing did not prevent a large number of schemes being discussed for the future of the site, ranging from demolition to radical reinvention, including converting the docks into a campus for Liverpool Polytechnic (now Liverpool John Moores University). The Mersey Docks and Harbour Board itself even considered demolition in 1960, and similar plans were still being hatched a decade later. Awarding conservation status to the Albert Dock in the 1970s brought proposals for big schemes to an end – replaced, unfortunately, by neglect and (that word again) dereliction. The advent in 1981 of the Merseyside Development Corporation, set up by the Conservative government as owner and planning authority for the Albert Dock site, set the wheels of regeneration turning. Slowly, the city had come to realise that its future depended partly on the careful protection of its heritage and that 'comprehensive redevelopment' was not necessarily the answer to its problems when buildings of architectural or historical merit were at stake. This, of course, raised the question of what heritage is for, prompting (as part of a more national programme of soul-searching) ideas about the provision of culture and the service economy – a concept which has latterly been joined by the term 'knowledge economy'. This thinking eventually led, in 1988, to both the Tate Gallery and Granada Television opening centres in the Albert Dock, while the remainder of the site's warehouses and administration buildings began to be kitted out as shops, cafes, bars and restaurants. Around 5 million people now visit the Albert Dock every year, making it the UK's third most popular tourist attraction. The docks, along with a significant parcel of land across Strand Street (including the Rope Walks district), were listed by UNESCO as a World Heritage Site in 2004 as 'the supreme example of a commercial port at the time of Britain's greatest global influence'.

At about the same time as the waterfront strategies began to bear fruit, a good deal more thinking was being devoted to the shabby hotchpotch of what should have been a splendid city core to the north. There was little point, after all, in creating a waterside leisure destination if people had to traverse a scruffy and unsafe district to get to it. Plus, there was that issue of inadequate shopping. A hefty report commissioned by the city council in 1998, and fully endorsed by councillors the following year, concluded (among many other things) that Liverpool was short of around 1 million square feet (93,000 square metres) of retail space; the report's authors, from property consultancy Healey & Baker (now part of Cushman & Wakefield), also concluded that the area around Paradise Street was a good place to put it.

The city had to renew the link with its waterfront and regain its status as the pre-eminent regional shopping destination

right
Bold Street, part of the Rope
Walks district, received considerable
attention in the 1990s, making the
streets safer and attracting private
developers. The area is now a
vibrant part of the city scene, with
strong connections with Grosvenor's
Liverpool One project.

far right
The Junction of Paradise Street
and Hanover Street, summer 2005.
In spite of the tragedy of war and
economic decline, Liverpool can still
boast a considerable number of fine
historic buildings. The curved shape
of this building, and others which
converge on this site, influenced the
form of the new John Lewis store.

'This level of floorspace is considered sustainable in retail capacity terms and desirable in securing the long-term regional status of Liverpool city centre,' said the report. 'The only site, in our view, which it is considered offers the opportunity to bring forward a scheme of this scale in a location which would fundamentally enhance the city centre as a whole is located at Paradise Street/ Bluecoat Triangle.' This would mean reversing the mistakes of the 1960s, including the demolition of the bus station and hotel, and virtually starting over.

Broadly, however, the city council already knew this. In fact, a dizzying number of initiatives, policies and action plans (drawn up by a multitude of agencies, partnerships and other interested parties) had begun to coalesce into an overall vision. Thinking at both national and regional level had come to regard city centres as the rightful place for retail development, as opposed to out-of-town shopping malls. During the 1990s, also, Liverpool City Council and other statutory authorities had identified the wider Rope Walks area for regeneration with a view to making it smarter, safer and attractive to investors. A move to give the area a make-over in the early 1990s broke down and the initiative was picked up later in the decade by architects BDP as part of a city council-sponsored, £150 million programme to improve the 'urban realm', deliver a smattering of new buildings and create job opportunities. This project met with considerable success, partly because of the fresh, no-nonsense approach taken by the architects: public squares were smartened up and new squares created by demolishing redundant buildings; lighting was improved; connecting streets were introduced where previously there had been none; elderly buildings were restored and updated; and financial help was given to developers when necessary (occasionally the cost of remaking a building would outweigh its final value). Significantly, people began to want to live in the area again.

The Albert Dock, with the Anglican
Cathedral beyond, in spring 2003.
The rejuvenation of the Albert Dock is
one of Liverpool's major achievements
in recent decades but, while popular,
these buildings remained cut off from
the rest of the city. Part of the city
council's brief to developers was to
create a stronger link between the
centre and the waterfront.

While this project was in progress, the area at its western edges began to receive special attention. This zone, around Paradise Street, lay adjacent to Liverpool's main shopping area and therefore offered the possibility of grandly extending the city's retail heart while reaching eastwards towards the clubs and bars of the Rope Walks proper. Instead of rehabilitation, Paradise Street and its environs probably needed an almost total reinvention. The promise of this area had been identified by the city council as early as 1993 and it was this potential that formed the focus of the retail study by Healey & Baker. At this point, the boundaries of the site which might accommodate a new shopping development weren't fixed – a core zone was pinpointed labelled the 'principal development area' (generally abbreviated to PDA in official documentation) while a looser, larger surrounding district called the Paradise Street Development Area (PSDA) was identified which also contained significant potential for a mix of uses including leisure facilities and housing. Surrounding that, in turn, was a fairly wide 'sphere of influence' comprising neighbouring parts of the city which would certainly feel the impact of a major new retail-led project in one way or another.

The determination to redevelop Paradise Street and its environs gained momentum as the new millennium approached, and the jargon and other nomenclature that began to appear in official circles border on the baffling. Quite apart from the PDA, the PSDA and a further zone known as the Main Retail Area (or MRA), there was a strategy document from the Northwest Regional Development Agency, an action plan called 'Liverpool First' from the Liverpool Partnership Group and a Strategic Development Framework from yet another agency called Liverpool Vision. This is all quite apart from the varying drafts of (and public inquiries into) the city council's Unitary Development Plan, a wide-ranging document that took seven years to finalise and sets out the planning agenda for the whole of Liverpool. This is not a complete list – there were also planning guidelines set at national level and a considerable amount of influential thinking (including the government's much publicised Urban White Paper of 2000) into how to secure the renaissance of inner cities. The language was visionary, aspirational, and often tough and pugnacious. There was a sense that the clock was ticking and that action was needed quickly if Liverpool was to face the new millennium with something to look forward to. Underlying all ideas for regeneration was the following principle: that any development should become an integral part of Liverpool and link almost seamlessly into the city as found. This was not to be a self-contained, inward-facing and self-absorbed scheme which would sit, shiny and in splendid isolation, as a distinct and separate part of Liverpool. The city already had a thriving but small shopping district, centred on Church

right
Hanover Street prior to Grosvenor's appointment and the advent of Liverpool One. Herbert the Hairdresser is now located in the distinctive 'Bling Bling' building by architects CZWG.

this page
Liverpool from across the Mersey.
The Liver Building is seen centre
left; the cranes to the right mark
the location of Grosvenor's activity
in the city.

Street, Lord Street and Parker Street, which should be enhanced rather than put out of business. Connections would have to be strengthened with other important districts – the Pier Head and its Three Graces, the waterfront, the railway stations, the universities and the residential buildings of the Rope Walks. It was all a very tall order, with a large number of important stakeholders. It was out of this highly charged and deeply political environment that the advertisement emerged in the summer of 1999 seeking private developers to reinvent a substantial chunk of the city centre, resulting in the appointment of Grosvenor the following year.

Liverpool Vision
Liverpool Vision, a 'delivery vehicle' for major developments, was formed as a partnership between Liverpool City Council, English Partnerships and the Northwest Regional Development Agency. That was in June 1999. A year later this new body published the final draft of its Strategic Regeneration Framework which provided the parameters against which major developments in the city could be measured.

'Liverpool led the world in the creation of public space and provided streets, squares and parks of the highest international quality. Today the city is indistinguishable from many other places,' said the document. 'A step change in the quality of public realm design, implementation and management must be made. This will have the fundamental benefit of radically improving the image of the city, stimulating investment and fostering civic pride. Liverpool must once again be seen to be a family friendly city to attract new residents, businesses and visitors and, not least, better serve the citizens of today.'

Brian Hatton, architect, academic and historian

The Origins of Liverpool

Passing through the new district of Liverpool One, walkers will encounter, just as they first see the warehouses of the Albert Dock, a circular balustrade surrounding a window in the pavement. Peering down into this unusual oculus, they will discern some stone ruins, exposed during the building of the new district. What they will be glimpsing, beneath the signs of renewal around them, are reminders of the origin of modern Liverpool – Thomas Steers's dock, opened in 1715.

Until construction of Steers's dock, Liverpool was but a score of streets on an exposed strand beside a muddy 'pool' in which a few ships could find haven. This unpromising creek was transformed by Steers and his backers (a combination of merchants and the town corporation) into the world's first commercial wet dock. Its shallows were excavated, its banks built up into masonry quays, and its shifting mouth deepened and secured by massive gates, open at high tide and closed at the ebb to harbour 50 ships. An immediate success, the dock became the focus of a web of new thoroughfares until, rendered obsolete by the other docks which it had spawned, its infilled basin became the foundation in the 1820s of Canning Place. At its centre was constructed, bigger than any other building in the now booming city, the new Custom House, domed and porticoed by architect John Foster to announce its national significance as the Exchequer's largest

single source of revenue – reflected in the fact that Liverpool had its own government office in Whitehall.

Canning Place was the centre of Georgian Liverpool for 120 years; but in May 1941 it suffered grievous bombing by the Luftwaffe. The dome of the Custom House was burned off so that its ruined rotunda became a circular courtyard open to the sky. In fact, the Blitz left the bulk of the Custom House, and much around it, intact and rebuildable; but in 1948 it was senselessly and expensively demolished by a philistine council. With its centrepiece gone, the rest of Canning Place was

pushed into irrevocable desolation. The Sailors' Home and other fine buildings went, and with the razing of South Castle Street and Sailmakers' Row its very identity as a 'place' was lost. With the abandonment, after 1970, of plans for an inner ring motorway the site was left for 30 years in a blighted limbo, barely ameliorated by its temporary designation as Chavasse Park. The blighting of Canning Place was one of the most disgraceful works of municipal misgovernance in 20th-century Britain. At last, Liverpool is beginning to redeem itself, starting with this most significant, abused and finally erased site: the original Pool itself.

Chapter 2
THE 'URBAN RENAISSANCE'

Chapter 2
THE 'URBAN RENAISSANCE'

The period in which Liverpool City Council began looking for a developer to rebuild the zone around Paradise Street was characterised by a great deal of national soul-searching and policy-making on the subject of urban design. It had come to be widely perceived that Britain's cities were being developed, if they were not being neglected, in a haphazard fashion. Everything from transport, planning policy, design, economics and the more human endeavours of 'place-making' were typically being considered in isolation, resulting in fragmented cities that lacked the cohesion and vitality of a previous age – or of other European cities such as Barcelona and Copenhagen. 'Many urban areas have suffered from neglect, poor management, inadequate public services, lack of investment and a culture of short-termism,' complained Deputy Prime Minister John Prescott in a government brochure entitled *Our Towns and Cities: the Future*, published in 2000.

The previous year had seen the publication of the landmark report *Towards an Urban Renaissance*, a wide-ranging and thoughtful study by Richard Rogers and a group of researchers called the Urban Task Force. This document, which contained more than 100 recommendations, argued that city developments should be designed more holistically (taking into account things like transport, safety, job creation and management all at once); local authorities should be more empowered and energetic with regard to regeneration schemes; tax incentives and public funding should be skewed towards the positive reinvention of urban spaces; while private funding should also be sought to create partnerships between the commercial and public sectors. Following this, the government's

right
The influences acting on Grosvenor's
central Liverpool development, the
border of which is outlined in red.
The development has come to act as
a hub, stitching the city back together
and linking its different districts.

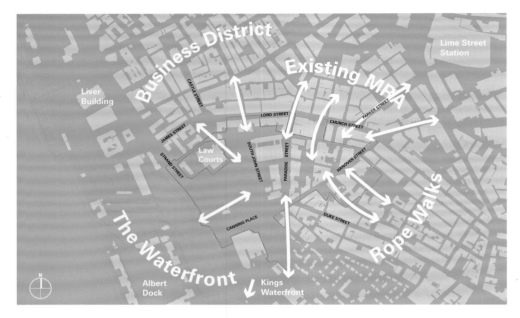

Commission for Architecture and the Built Environment issued an influential booklet with the mouthful of a title *By Design: urban planning in the design system – towards better practice*. This, too, sought to join the dots between vastly different disciplines, such as design and economics, while making the case for the importance of context and considering the needs of people. 'Good urban design is essential if we are to produce attractive, high-quality, sustainable places in which people will want to live, work and relax,' said the foreword to the report. 'It is fundamental to our objective of an urban renaissance. We do not have to put up with shoddy, unimaginative and second-rate buildings and urban areas. There is a clamour for better designed places which inspire and can be cherished, places where vibrant communities can grow and prosper.' Success, the authors argued, depended on four main factors:

• a clear development and planning framework from the local authority;
• a sensitive response to local context;
• a realistic understanding of economic and market conditions;
• an imaginative and appropriate design approach from both designers and planners.

Officials within Liverpool City Council, with their private sector and government agency advisers, were clearly being influenced by this new thinking and the development brief for Paradise Street embodied much (if not all) of this new agenda. Potential developers were asked to consider *simultaneously* design quality, heritage, retail provision, car parking, public transport, pedestrian links, access, sustainability, vitality, overall visual appeal and financial viability. Such was the challenge that only large, well-resourced and technically sophisticated developers were able to respond. Grosvenor, however, needed little convincing that this all-encompassing approach was the right one.

'The proposition back in 1999 and 2000 was that if the city could do a deal with the private property sector, it might be possible to regenerate the city from the centre and build outwards. All the good, well-intentioned and important work that had gone on before – such as the rescue and restoration

above
Liverpool always had a retail centre
– it was just not large enough for
the city's catchment area. This view,
of Church Street, shows how an
arcade has been created through
a pre-existing building to create
a new link with Grosvenor's
development beyond.

above
Early sketch from BDP of how the
new retail development might look.
This was going to be a district of
streets and squares – not a mall.

above right
South John Street in its earliest
incarnation. The multi-layered nature
of the street and the gentle curve
suggested in this sketch are a close
match with the finished project.

of the Albert Dock and the Garden Festival – weren't changing anything much. It wasn't reversing what seemed to be the terminal decline of Liverpool. The idea emerged that the city had to start again from the centre,' said Rod Holmes, Grosvenor's project director for Liverpool One. 'We understood the proposition immediately. At its heart was a hugely ambitious vision that Liverpool could be turned around and dragged up from its miserable position at the bottom of the league of major European cities – a bit player on the fringe of a thriving continent. It was the notion that it might be possible to change the fortunes of the city by reactivating its centre.'

That the city council wanted to enter into a partnership with the private sector was entirely in accordance with the principles set out in the urban renaissance agenda. Liverpool was also ready for it. After Militant lost its grip on the city in the late 1980s, a more pragmatic Labour Party leadership began to build bridges with the private sector, a move that was strengthened when a Liberal Democrat administration replaced Labour in 1998. 'You can't badmouth the private sector and then expect them to invest in your city,' comments Jack Stopforth, chief executive of the local Chamber of Commerce.

Liverpudlians now observe that their city's troubled decades of decline and under-investment have worked in its favour; while other cities had been quietly getting on with it, Liverpool's turn for renewal occurred at a time when urban design and regeneration had risen to the top of the political and architectural agendas. Because so little had happened in the city for so long, Liverpool was taking a single, dramatic leap forward at exactly the same time as urban design had reached a whole new level of sophistication. 'It was an important stroke of luck,' says Stopforth. Liverpool became a test-bed for a whole new design vocabulary (words like 'connectivity' came into vogue) and all eyes were trained on the city to see what would happen. 'We have set the agenda for city centre development, there is no doubt about that. We've had a constant stream of architects and other developers up here to see what we're doing,' said Rod Holmes long before the development was complete.

above

As well as a commitment to open spaces and 'connectivity', Grosvenor insisted on architectural variety. Here, the work of at least three firms of architects can be seen.

Retail-led regeneration

'Shopping is the UK's national pastime,' begins a 2007 study into the future of retail property, written for the British Council of Shopping Centres by Grosvenor's group research director Richard Barkham. 'The average person makes an annual 200 trips to the shops. It is difficult to overstate the importance of retailing to the UK's economic and social well-being, or its significance to a very wide range of public and private sector interests. The facts and figures speak for themselves: not only do retail sales account for approximately 21% of Gross Domestic Product, but shops play a central role in shaping the places and communities that influence people's everyday lives.'

If shops are so important they obviously have to be in the right place, of the right mix and of sufficient quality to be economically sustainable (that is, profitable over the long term). That has always been the case, of course, but retail development has been brought very firmly into the sphere of 'urban renaissance' and 'city living' thinking explained above. Shopping as a pastime, rather than an unpleasant necessity, requires that retailers become part of the leisure business; shopping districts have to become wonderful places to be, especially if people want to go to the trouble of personally buying a product rather than ordering it up at the click of a mouse. Shopping centres are becoming places to eat, and longer opening hours mix shoppers with late-night revellers, blurring the boundaries between day-time and night-time economies. They might also be places for people to live, adding a sense of community 'ownership' to a place and preventing retail quarters from becoming abandoned and frightening when the 'Closed' signs finally go up. That is the point of retail-led regeneration – retail leads the development but does not have an exclusive hold over it.

'Place-making must be an overarching objective, involving identity and community building through the creation of vital and highly differentiated spaces,' says Barkham's report, which drew on what Grosvenor had learned in Liverpool. 'Diversity must evolve in terms of architectural style, treatment of buildings, the mixture of uses, treatment of the public realm, new technologies, and dynamic place-management and brand identity.' The study then goes on to list the kind of thing which makes retail development successful in the 21st century: a mix of retailers, not restricted to fashion outlets; character, identity and even iconic design; safe, relaxing public spaces; integration with surrounding streets; and connections with multiple modes of transport. The design of shopping districts is, evidently, no different from good urban design generally. Indeed, good urban design and commercial principles are not incompatible.

Planning policy at both national and regional level specifies that shopping developments should be built in town centres if at all possible, and that only when searches for central urban sites have been exhausted should edge-of-town plots, or even out-of-town sites, be considered. The reasons for this should be self-evident. Town centres rely on shops (plus other leisure facilities like restaurants and cinemas) for life and vitality, and they become sterile without them. Too many out-of-town shopping malls – with their convenience, weather-proofed and climate-controlled interiors, and ample parking provision – have rendered town centres almost meaningless. The term 'centre' becomes a geographical description only. Good shopping also generates confidence, wealth and high rents for an urban centre, which can in turn attract other employers who wish to locate themselves in an area perceived as thriving and worthy of investment. However, large inner city developments can be problematic because large plots rarely have a single owner, making land assembly troublesome and expensive; also, out-of-town (especially greenfield) sites involve the developer in fewer contextual issues and they are freer to build an enclosed box without fretting over matters such as scale and integration. City centre schemes, especially ones the size of Liverpool One, need bold commercial developers and committed civic leaders in order to succeed.

All policy development in Liverpool throughout the 1990s concluded that the city needed to revitalise its centre with a retail-led scheme, not least because the range, scale and location of its shopping facilities were so poor. In the early 1970s Liverpool ranked third in a list of the country's

right
John Lewis, on the left of this picture, was always designed to be highly permeable – accessible at a number of levels and from all sides.

Mike Storey

The council leader
1998–2006

The immensity of the Liverpool One project is such that its success or failure can never be placed at the feet of a single individual. Mike Storey, however, is certainly one of the very few people who can claim to have made an absolutely overwhelming contribution to this development's delivery. It was down to Storey, then leader of Liverpool City Council, that Grosvenor was appointed at all. Towards the end of 1999 six developers of international standing had been shortlisted for the job of redeveloping Paradise Street and its environs, and during early 2000 this number was whittled down to just two – Grosvenor and Hammerson. A council selection committee of four elected councillors, which met on 6 March, was split down the middle. Storey and another Liberal Democrat colleague favoured Grosvenor, while Hammerson's proposal appealed to a further Liberal Democrat and a Labour councillor. The meeting was adjourned and Sir David Henshaw, then chief executive of the city council, suggested that Storey should make the call. 'I just felt more comfortable with Grosvenor's approach. I liked the scheme and the people,' Storey remembers. 'We went back to the meeting and talked it through. It was all very affable and the other members said they would make my decision unanimous.'

Storey, a primary school teacher since 1990, became leader of the city council after the local elections in 1998. This election saw power in the city transferred from the Labour Party to the Liberal

Democrats and Storey quickly began to draw up an agenda for Liverpool. It was odd, he thought, that a city that was mad on music didn't have an arena in which bands could perform to large audiences (a 10,000-seat venue has since been built on the Kings Waterfront); second, it was equally odd that a city that had such a close relationship with the sea

didn't have a cruise liner terminal (which it now has); finally, it was painfully obvious that the city's core shopping centre was in decline. Culture-led regeneration, being pursued by cities such as Bilbao and Newcastle/Gateshead, never featured on the agenda. 'Why would we go for culture-led regeneration? We've got a big enough cultural offer as it is,' says Storey.

The retail study of 1999 merely confirmed what the city council already suspected – that Liverpool could accommodate much more retail space and that the logical step forward was to expand the shopping zones around Church and Lord Streets rather than build a new centre somewhere else. Storey was adamant that he didn't want a mall and that existing street patterns should be more or less respected. 'We always saw the city centre as hugely important to the city of Liverpool. It was the engine, the powerhouse for the city and the wider region,' says Storey. 'And we were always very, very clear that we were never, ever, going to commission a giant mall.'

Storey also comments that Liverpool One has been such a success in design, commercial and political terms because of the close working relationship between the city council and Grosvenor. Back in 1999 the council tried to impress upon developers that it wanted to appoint a partner instead of a scheme, and Grosvenor rather took them at their word. Councillors sat in on regular design meetings and their comments, queries and naïve observations were taken seriously. 'This wasn't just lip service,' insists Storey, who adds that architects were replaced 'more than once' when design committees felt they were unable to respond to the brief in a satisfactory way.

Storey relishes one particular moment when he stopped Sir Jeremy Dixon in his tracks. One of the more elegant and finely tuned elements within Liverpool One is Dixon Jones Architects' covered arcade for Peter's Lane. During a presentation by the practice, Storey interrupted with a comment that his proposal looked like a garage lock-up. Dixon was visibly disconcerted and telephoned the following day with an invitation to guide Storey around some of his completed schemes in London. Only after the tour, did Storey feel able to give the scheme his backing.

Although Liverpool One is the result of a close partnering between the city council and Grosvenor, the relationship was also characterised by tough and often difficult negotiations. Happily, it appears that both parties were evenly matched. Storey believes that Grosvenor was probably 'rather shocked' by the council's ability to drive a commercial bargain (especially via the city's regeneration chief Charlie Parker), while he concedes that Grosvenor, too, was no push-over. Rod Holmes in particular, he recalls, was 'very, very tough in negotiations' and conceals behind his courteous and respectful demeanour a 'rod of steel'. Mercifully, both Grosvenor and the city council appear to have struck the right balance between commercial return and public service. 'This is the largest single development in Liverpool's history. That's a huge responsibility for Grosvenor and the city. And Grosvenor has got it right,' says Storey.

Better still, Storey believes that Liverpool One has made local people feel better about themselves. Over a period of 20 or 30 years, he says, Liverpudlians felt demoralised. Unemployment reached rates of 30 per cent in some districts as large employers like Tate & Lyle and Dunlop closed factories. There was also an embarrassing catalogue of unfortunate events which suggested that Liverpool was synonymous with bad news: the Toxteth riots of 1981; the Heysel Stadium disaster four years later in which Liverpool fans were implicated in the deaths of 39 (mainly Italian) football supporters in Brussels; the 1989 Hillsborough disaster in which 96 Liverpool fans lost their lives in Sheffield; the murder of three-year-old James Bulger in 1993. 'There was a sense of victimhood about the city. People became very introspective,' says Storey. 'And then for the first time in living memory Liverpool was getting serious investment. International developers were coming along saying "We want to invest in your city". That was unheard of. I think Liverpool is genuinely proud of what has been achieved.'

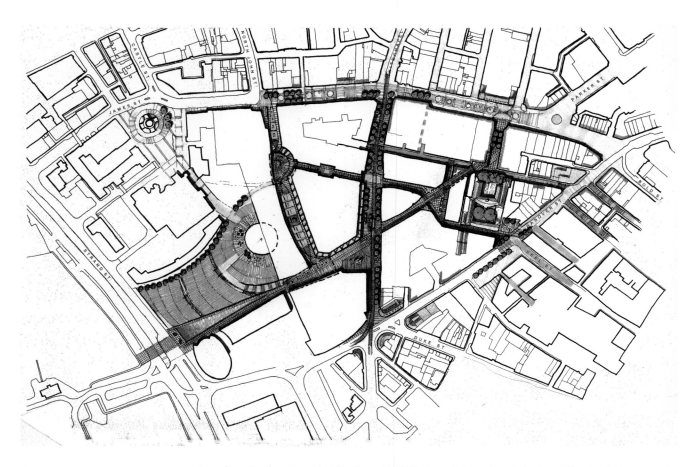

above

In this masterplanning sketch,
the broad moves of the design can
be seen: the street connections,
the park and the variation in scale.
At this stage, however, the grand
elliptical gestures are absent and the
location of the bus station is unclear.

prime shopping locations, but by the mid-1990s it had slipped to 17th place. The city had managed to keep the rents of its 'prime pitch' reasonably high, but this was merely a matter of supply and demand; the prime pitch itself was relatively small. At the turn of the millennium Liverpool had 21 shops that were paying at least 90 per cent of the rent for a prime pitch site, while the national average was 43 shops. There were also fewer shops overall – 688 shops in the city centre, compared with more than 900 in Manchester and nearly 1,500 in Glasgow. In comparison with Nottingham the city came off particularly badly – Nottingham could boast around 1,150 shops for a catchment area that is not only smaller than Liverpool's but includes Leicester, which has its own shopping centre. Liverpool's shops were also smaller than the national average, while fashion retailers were largely limited to budget and mid-range stores, with few luxury brand names available. And to make matters worse, the city's provision for good, large 'anchor stores' was poor – Marks & Spencer had (and still has) a reasonable presence in the centre, but a John Lewis store was small and awkward. A House of Fraser operation had closed and it was not inconceivable that John Lewis would also have left the city had it not eventually taken up a flagship position in the new Liverpool One development. There was one more problem with Liverpool's shopping facilities: partly because of the way the city had developed historically, and partly because of postwar development, its retail district was very linear, extending up Lord Street through Church Street and Parker Street and into Bold Street. There was very little of interest on either side of this ribbon of shops, and this single stretch offered little variation in character or scale; there was not a great deal of exploration to be done, and the adventurous shopper would quickly return to the principal stretch. The number of people shopping on side streets was significantly less than along that main route. By the mid-1990s officials and consultants began to worry that this poor provision would, with little or no investment, lead to decline – that the stores the city did have would begin to suffer if too many people decided to shop elsewhere.

'Liverpool city centre's main retail area has significantly reduced in influence within the region and its nationwide ranking as a centre has fallen significantly. Its market share is projected to decrease further by 2006 and 2011 if action is not taken to remedy the situation,' stated the Healey & Baker report on retail provision, submitted to the city council in February 1999. The nub of the problem was that Liverpool had suffered from a lack of retail investment over many years while other regional centres had seen 'significant development' in this regard. Furthermore, the report continued, the view of shoppers, retailers and investors was that Liverpool's main retail area was unwelcoming, unsafe, dirty and of poor quality, a perception that made affluent people at the city's edge less likely to shop there.

The ambition was for a massive extension to what Liverpool already offered, but of higher quality, broader appeal, better served and integrated into what was already there

The proposed solution was ambitious and wide-ranging: a 1.65 million square foot (approximately 154,000 square metre) retail and leisure development 'anchored' by two premier league department stores; a good range of 'semi-anchors' (smaller retailers with strong, desirable brands); speciality shops and a good number of independent retailers; a fuller range of fashion and catering outlets, across all price sectors and appealing to the widest number of people; and shops offering goods and services that are not available in smaller shopping centres. The vision also included 2 hotels, residential and office space, better car parking, vastly improved public transport and a high quality public realm. The ambition was for a massive new extension to what Liverpool already had to offer, but of higher quality with a superior mix, broader appeal, better served and integrated into what was already there. In short, Liverpool wanted to be put back on the map. 'The council wishes to see design proposals which provide an external, visible and self-advertising facade, provide a new external vision for the city centre and raise the profile of the city centre both nationally and internationally,' announced the brief to interested developers.

Significantly, all the figures showed that demand from both retailers and consumers was there for such a large retail expansion – rents in the prime pitch were actually rising because of the lack of space, while studies into customer spending patterns showed that Liverpool and its environs had the wealth that could sustain the shops being planned. The problem was not that large numbers of people in and around the city were short of money; it was just that they had started to shop elsewhere. The fact that Liverpool's prime pitch was so close to such under-utilised land was plain odd.

The appointment of Grosvenor

Having worked so hard at policy level for so long, the time came for Liverpool City Council to bite the bullet and start to make the vision a reality. An advertisement appeared in the national property press in the summer of 1999 asking developers to express an interest. There was then nothing for city leaders and officials to do but wait – anxiously. 'We were sitting here in depressed Liverpool wondering if anyone would be interested. And then 47 developers expressed an interest. We thought "wow"', remembers Michael Burchnall, the city's planning chief. He needn't have been so surprised. Healey & Baker (the firm had been retained as consultants by the city council) had been speaking informally to developers three or four months in advance of the advertisement's publication; the property industry knew it was coming.

right
Vistas and glimpses of city landmarks were built into the masterplan from the start. Here, a drawing from Pelli Clarke Pelli indicates the intention to offer views of the Three Graces from across the renewed Chavasse Park.

Liverpool One   Remaking a city centre

Grosvenor was one of the 47. Encouraged by the sea change in local politics and the city's obvious determination to press ahead with radical change, it pitched in with fund manager Henderson Investors as a joint venture. 'What we were interested in, and were actually becoming very passionate about, was the regeneration of city centres. We saw Liverpool as an extraordinary city, a city with the most impressive historic content. But it had been badly neglected and bombing had left a hole in its centre. I knew that if we could fill in the middle we'd be creating one of the most wonderful cities in the UK – if we got the quality right,' says Stephen Musgrave, formerly chief executive of Grosvenor Great Britain & Ireland, now CEO of property firm Hines UK.

Musgrave, with Grosvenor's then retail chief John Bullough, set about the project with a determination that went beyond commercial imperatives. They'd caught something of the zeal for transformation projected by Liverpool's council leaders. 'These people were driving change and were, amazingly, shifting this place where almost nothing had happened for 30 years. Their infectious belief that things were going to change was inspiring,' remembers Bullough. 'I sat everybody down in a room and told them that we would win this, that we didn't lose competitions.'

An outline development brief was issued to shortlisted companies the following October. Grosvenor found itself lined up against six other developers: Hammerson; Capital Shopping Centres; Australian firm Westfield; Dutch company MDC; a Land Securities/Lend Lease joint

above
The masterplan included the provision for two or three large department stores – an essential part of the retail strategy. Signing John Lewis, seen in the background, was crucial to the success of the development.

left
A pair of arcades provides important connections from Church Street through to the heart of the new retail zone. The arcade in the foreground ends with a small square; a further arcade lies on the other side. At first the suggestion of arcades made the city council nervous; officials wanted to avoid anything suggestive of a mall.

venture; and Peel Holdings (which eventually pulled out of the process). Submissions, which had to be in the hands of the city council by 17 December, were then presented and scrutinised in early 2000 at a series of technical workshops, attended not only by the city council but by other agencies including Merseytravel, Liverpool Vision and English Heritage. Even at this early stage it was clear that this would be one of the most significant development projects of the coming decade, perhaps longer, and the city was determined to get this right. Great efforts were made to be as clean, honest and transparent as possible. 'It was a very well-run developer competition,' recalls Rod Holmes. 'It was very tough, because a lot of people wanted it and we all took it very seriously. It was fought extremely hard.'

Holmes joined the Grosvenor team as project director on the eve of Grosvenor's shortlisting. He had a reputation as a tenacious, straight-talking, very driven individual. Stephen Musgrave remembers sitting down with Holmes in the hope that he could tempt him away from Dutch developer MAB. 'I said to him, "Rod, I can't offer you a title, or even the same amount of money you're getting now, but I can offer you a hell of a job." We needed somebody who would devote their life to the project.' The appointment was inspired. Holmes brought with him continental ideas about both city living and project management, as well as an obsession with quality and an unusually acute architectural sensibility. He has had nothing less than a profound effect on the way Liverpool's ambitions have come to fruition. At the opening of Phase One of the development on 29 May 2008,

Liverpool City Council needed a partner from the private sector that would look far beyond the immediate horizon

city council leader Warren Bradley took the microphone and called Holmes 'heroic'. Everybody who had anything to do with the project knew what he meant. Throughout his involvement (from October 1999 to December 2008, when he retired) Holmes lived and breathed Liverpool One.

On 6 March 2000, after delivering what John Bullough remembers as 'a grilling beyond grillings', the city council announced that Grosvenor/Henderson had been selected as its 'preferred development partner'. The wording is important. The city council was not looking for a fully worked out solution; rather, it sought a developer with whom it could work over the long term. The council wanted a developer rather than a design, and the fine detail could wait; the project would undoubtedly

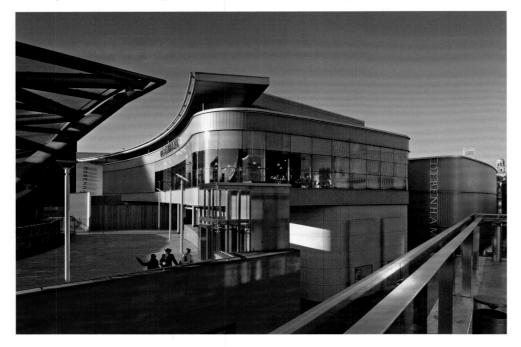

require the use of compulsory purchase orders, the Paradise Street Development Framework had
yet to be fully ratified and there was even a rival scheme being proposed on part of the development
area which would have to be fought in the courts. In early 2000, all the council wanted was to find a
developer who could, first, deliver the right scheme and, second, empathise with the brief – at least
one didn't, and proposed an enclosed shopping mall as a *fait accompli*. 'Some presented schemes you
could start building tomorrow. Grosvenor didn't,' remembers the city council's Michael Burchnall.
'The Grosvenor scheme was an interesting one. It wasn't as developed as the others, but it embodied
some interesting principles ... that was a key factor.' It was also about trust and personalities.
Everyone concerned knew that, once the appointment had been made, relationships would have
to survive many years of stresses and strains. Failure was too appalling an idea to contemplate and
the city council needed to know that Grosvenor would never walk away before the job was finished.
Commissioning Grosvenor wasn't just a commercial decision; it was deeply personal.

Grosvenor always knew where the city council was coming from. For a start, after developing
Mayfair and Belgravia the company had managed its London estate for more than 300 years;
Grosvenor therefore understood that high quality and a good financial return were not mutually

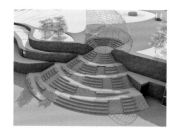

above
At one stage in the evolution of the project, the grand steps to Chavasse Park contained a series of ramps. This was one of many iterations of this element of the scheme. The entire site contains a fall of 36 feet (11 metres), and the design team worked hard to ensure this awkward topography was dealt with as simply and elegantly as possible.

left
These circular steps into Chavasse Park have a solidity that gives the impression they have been carved from the bedrock of Liverpool. The use of long-lasting materials and a commitment to quality have become hallmarks of this project.

exclusive. Beyond that, the idea of investing for the very long term had become part of Grosvenor's value system; Liverpool was never going to be a quick fix and the city council (keen to end its culture of dependence and replace public subsidy with investment) needed a partner from the private sector that would look far beyond the immediate horizon. Developing inner city sites is an expensive business, not least because of the price of land, while the cost and complexity of integrating buildings with the transport and street/services infrastructure add significantly to the economics of a project. Getting a return on the sort of investment necessary is always going to mean taking the long view, and Grosvenor was literally the only developer that could offer this sort of pedigree. 'You can't divorce yourself from history,' says Grosvenor's then group chief executive Jeremy Newsum. 'Over 340 years, someone has worked with someone who worked with someone right back to the beginning. There is still a resonance in the company with what we have created in London. Liverpool is a great expression of our values.'

Also working in the company's favour was the fact that, quite apart from building and managing some of London's premier neighbourhoods for so long, since the 1960s Grosvenor had built up a strong track record in delivering shopping centres around the UK; by the time Liverpool City Council was looking for a developer, Grosvenor had built 5 million square feet (465,000 square metres) of retail space across 16 centres and was in the process of developing a further retail-led project in Cambridge. The quickest and cheapest way to fill the physical and retail void represented by Paradise Street would have been to build a covered mall, but Grosvenor resisted this option almost instinctively; there was a business case to answer, of course, but the company seized the opportunity Liverpool was offering as a chance to show what it was capable of. It is no coincidence that in 2000 the company restructured and a new top team was in place, keen to demonstrate its expertise.

Energising the centre
Rod Holmes, project director, Grosvenor
The basic idea was that Liverpool's long-term decline could be turned round by re-creating the very heart of the city centre around the place where the spectacular growth of the great city and port started 300 years ago – the site of the world's first commercial dock. Together with Mike Storey, council leader at the time, we figured that if enough private investment and creative energy could be injected into that place, then it would encourage other businesses and investors to look at Liverpool afresh, while we directly created jobs and the feel-good factor, re-establishing the city as a premier league shopping, leisure and tourism destination.

We started with the existing street pattern and the 'grain' of the city, determined to keep the shopping area as compact as possible, using the natural topography of the headland where the sandstone castle once stood, and the course of the creek (the Pool), now Paradise Street, wrapped around it. We would create truly 'city streets' with tall, majestic buildings by leading architects, of our own time but worthy of the heritage around them.

We set out to demonstrate the confidence, creativity and pride that we believed lay dormant in this great city. We believed we could draw on it by involving the people in our ideas and process, by learning Liverpool's history and trying to get beneath its skin, so that what we produced would be as unique and special as its inheritances.

The choice of Grosvenor was a close call, however. The city council selection panel was split right down the middle and it was up to council leader Mike Storey to make a decision and break the impasse. As described on page 44 Storey selected Grosvenor based on a judgement about the company's integrity: it was a matter of people, personality and values. 'I liked the fact that Grosvenor's approach was so closely matched with my own thinking at the time, and it's a decision I've never regretted,' says Storey. 'There are moments in life when the time is right, the people are right and the circumstances are right. It all came down to Grosvenor.'

But why get involved at all? The city council was able to paint a convincing picture of undersupply and opportunity, but did Liverpool stack up as a business proposition for Grosvenor? Because of the city's recent economic and social history, there was a good deal of cynicism to overcome and would-be investors had to set aside prejudice and examine hard facts. All the research, including a series of studies undertaken by (or commissioned by) Grosvenor, reached similar conclusions to that of the city council and its advisers. Surveys of thousands of local people indicated that there was indeed a considerable potential for more retail facilities in central Liverpool; retailers themselves also agreed, and by the time Grosvenor was appointed the company had established good reasons to think that it could reach around £300 per square foot (0.09 square metres) for prime retail space (roughly what was being achieved in nearby Church Street). A later report by Drivers Jonas dated January 2001 lent further support to the weight of evidence that had been massing in favour of the comprehensive redevelopment of the Paradise Street area. The study reported that Liverpool city centre was attracting far too few people from its potential catchment

Absolute commitment

'Grosvenor Developments Ltd and Henderson ... believe that the [Paradise Street] project presents a wonderful opportunity to create a unique, mixed-use development which will not only transform this area of the city and strengthen linkages with adjoining districts but will also act as a catalyst for wider regeneration, bringing major new employment to the city and setting a benchmark for the next generation of city centre development,' read the introduction to Grosvenor's expression of interest document, submitted to Liverpool City Council in August 1999.

'We have assembled a professional team of the highest calibre which is well equipped to address, from a strong local base, the complex problems which will inevitably arise. With regard to these challenges, team working will be essential and we envisage Liverpool City Council and its representatives as being key members of the team. We place great importance on the value of public consultation and would wish to work in partnership with representatives of the local community to produce a development with which local people will closely identify and take to their hearts.

'We know from experience that city centre development projects such as Bluecoat Triangle will require a long-term commitment which we are prepared to make. We believe that we have not only the skills to deliver a project of the highest order to be worthy of the city of Liverpool but also the financial means to ensure that it can be delivered. We are highly selective about the development opportunities we seek and do not register our interest in this project lightly. We have considered carefully the responsibility and implications it carries as well as the opportunity it represents and, as a result, we are now resolved absolutely to secure this project.'

above
Paradise Street. This is the
principal street running through
the development, defined by large
buildings and long views. This
pedestrian street terminates with
the John Lewis department store
and the bus station.

area, and went on to predict that the project would increase the number of shoppers so much that annual turnover in the main retail area would multiply to the tune of hundreds of millions of pounds. Largely, this would be because wealthy people who had moved to the fringes of the city would be tempted to shop there again. 'There was a lot of money clearly leaking out of the centre which should have been spent there,' says Rod Holmes.

Further data compiled by Grosvenor's in-house research team throughout 2003, when the company was approaching investors, showed that Liverpool's economy was not only stabilising but reviving: unemployment was declining; growth was accelerating; tourist numbers were increasing; the number of people living in the centre of the city was rising; while the sales and rental growth for the Paradise Street area was predicted to grow steadily. Figures from the *National Survey of Local*

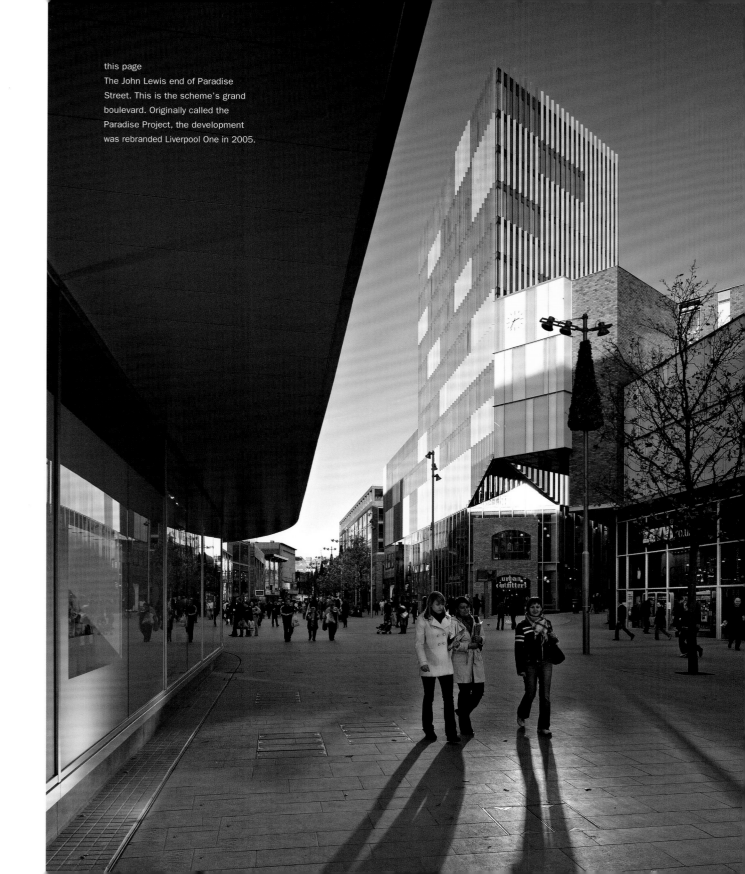

this page
The John Lewis end of Paradise
Street. This is the scheme's grand
boulevard. Originally called the
Paradise Project, the development
was rebranded Liverpool One in 2005.

below
Computer model of central Liverpool,
emphasising the connectivity of
the masterplan. The intention was
always to allow people to pass
through the development without
corralling them in cul-de-sacs.

Shopping Patterns, produced by property consultancy CB Richard Ellis, also showed that while 690,000 people fell within Liverpool's 'core' catchment area (only half of whom actually shopped there), the city had a 'secondary' catchment area of nearly 2 million people if smaller centres such as Chester, Warrington, Crewe and Southport were included. Extending this catchment area to include 'tertiary' zones like north Wales and population centres northwards around the M6 Motorway would create a potential market of almost 4.7 million people. And, according to the predictions, all these markets (core, secondary and tertiary) were set to grow. Planning consultants Drivers Jonas conducted a detailed analysis of spending patterns and calculated that, for the year 2008, more than £800 million of shoppers' money would be available for an expanded retail district.

below
Computer model of central Liverpool, emphasising the connectivity of the masterplan. The intention was always to allow people to pass through the development without corralling them in cul-de-sacs.

right
View across Liverpool One towards
the Mersey. The John Lewis building,
designed by John McAslan + Partners,
can be seen at the bottom centre of
the picture.

Alistair Parker, partner, Cushman & Wakefield
Looking back to the start of what must be the most extraordinary city-centre renewal
project since the postwar reconstruction, one wonders where the audacity, the civic
determination, the commercial vigour and the personal ambitions came from. Dusting
off the early files, one is struck by the cascade of seemingly unrelated events that,
collectively, led disparate actors to come together to form a powerful partnership
for change.

For the city council, the key impetus came when the Liberal Democrats, led by Mike
Storey, took over in May 1998. They were determined to revive the city but not with just
any development. They would not accept an enclosed, semi-private and inward-looking
shopping mall disconnected from the surrounding city streets. Despite calls in the early
1990s for permeable, mixed-use schemes, the property industry was generally hostile
to the idea. We were not. When we wrote the briefs for the developer competition,
the requirement for open streets was clearly set out. Despite that, five out of seven
of the UK's leading development companies came forward with mono-cultural lumps.
Grosvenor, by contrast, saw different mixed-use quarters centred on open streets
framed by different buildings. And, in 2000, we would never have been able to sell
a partnership with the City without the remarkable organisational re-engineering that
the council's CEO Sir David Henshaw brought about.

Most of all, one is struck by the social commitment made by Grosvenor and by the
Duke of Westminster to his regional roots; a commitment to delivery and to the high
standards promised at the very outset. Almost precisely 10 years after it began,
Liverpool One has fulfilled all that was promised.

The whole business proposition came down to three main factors: the revived spending power of local consumers; the demand for space from retailers; and the anticipated rental growth. All these indicators pointed in the right direction.

That Liverpool was later to be designated European Capital of Culture for 2008 was also to prove persuasive because the title had clearly benefited Glasgow so much in 1990: that city had experienced an 81 per cent rise in visitor numbers, as well as 5,600 new jobs and a major change of image. At the time, Liverpool confidently expected that its turn as culture capital would deliver similar (if not better) results.

The development brief issued by the city council was, by common consent, excellent. But it was purely aspirational

top

An early incarnation of the park's profile, showing a gentle sweep upwards. At this stage of the design process, the design of One Park West had yet to be resolved.

above

This later elevation of the park shows how the landscape has been bulked out, creating a more level surface towards the top of the park. It has become more of a plateau than a wedge.

All the figures, then, stacked up and Liverpool genuinely appeared to be a sound investment opportunity. 'If you find something at rock bottom but on the up, that's attractive in development terms,' explains Grosvenor's Jeremy Newsum, who remembers the company looking into the potential of Liverpool long before the city council began the search for a development partner. Liverpool was on Grosvenor's business radar as early as 1997, which was why it responded so quickly and effectively to the call for developers two years later. That said, personal motivations were also at work. The Duke of Westminster's Eaton estate near Chester and close to Liverpool, has been in the family for centuries; the Duke, who is the shareholder of the Grosvenor business and who was until 2007 non-executive chairman of the Grosvenor Group, has long been associated with Liverpool and his charitable foundation has been particularly active there. Indeed, he says that Liverpool is the city he knows best, after London and Chester. Not only were the economic indicators right for investment, then, but investing in Liverpool also felt good. 'But the only case that mattered was the business case,' Newsum emphasises. 'We have a rule that no single project or activity can in any way jeopardise the whole group.'

Development of the masterplan

The development brief issued by the city council was, by common consent, excellent, but it is important to understand that the brief was purely aspirational – effectively a detailed shopping list. What Grosvenor and its consultants did was take this list and add to it, turning aspirations and requirements into plans and massing studies. With its newly assembled masterplanning team, plans evolved which modulated the scale and grain of the development, building up from the smaller, more intimate streetscape of the Rope Walks to something of the grandeur of the Pier Head. (The masterplanning team, identified as early as August 1999, comprised: BDP, masterplanners; Symonds Group, transportation consultants; Drivers Jonas, planning consultants; PMA property research consultants; and Strutt & Parker, retail consultants and one of the letting agents.) Key views were also factored into the plans, ensuring that local landmarks like the Liver Building and the Albert Dock were framed by new buildings. The entire development was to be conceived along the lines of what Grosvenor calls 'living cities', an idea that chimes with the Richard Rogers' and urban renaissance agenda outlined above. 'From Day One everyone had a common goal', remembers Terry Davenport of BDP. 'The city council, the design team and Grosvenor all knew that this would be an exemplar project in terms of all the thinking emerging at the same time. Nobody ever questioned that.'

Most architects will agree that the best projects come out of intelligent responses to constraints. Rather than building in a vacuum, in which almost anything can happen, design teams genuinely need something to respond to. With the wrong attitude these contextual, financial and functional demands can be seen as obstacles to creative expression; but given a positive spin they become starting points on which to hang ideas. Constraints are potentially, therefore, a good thing. And Liverpool presented plenty of them. In practical, physical terms the biggest constraint was arguably the topography of the site. The inlet on which the early city was built once flowed right into the middle of what is now the development area, wrapping around a small headland, now Derby Square. There is a 36 foot (11 metre) difference in height between Derby Square and dock-level

right
This drawing shows how the masterplan developed after US firm Pelli Clarke Pelli joined the masterplanning team. The park and surrounding buildings have become defined by dramatic arcs.

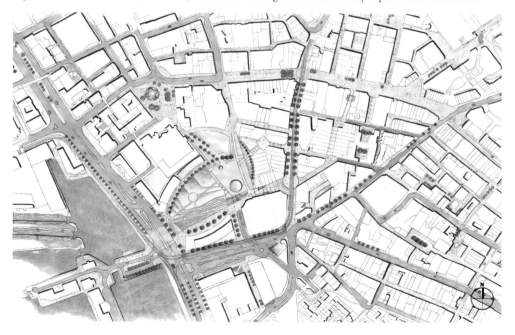

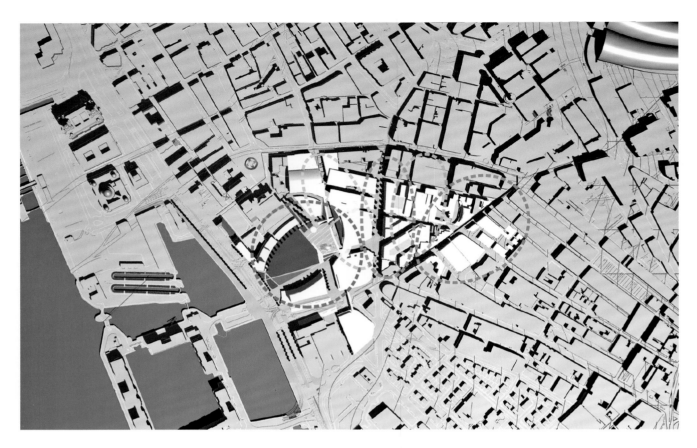

Rather than considering the
development as a single retail zone,
Grosvenor developed the idea of
creating distinct 'districts'. Each
district would have its own flavour,
and allow the scale of the design to
step down from the grand gesture
at its western end to smaller and
narrower spaces at its east, where
the development meets the historic
Bluecoat building.

Canning Place and the design team was anxious to negotiate these contours comfortably while
including the provision for public transport, car parking and open space. Basic economics also
dictated the number and size of shops that should be accommodated, while fundamental retail
planning principles (such as separating large 'anchor' stores in order to encourage people to walk
past the smaller shops ranged between them) also had to be factored in. Eventually, during the
summer of 2000, the team managed to turn this topography to its advantage. The idea hinged on
bringing Chavasse Park, open ground created from a Second World War bomb site, within the
boundary of the development (at the time the park lay just outside the PSDA boundary and was
the subject of a separate retail proposal by the Walton Group). If the park could be raised, that
would free up space for 2,000 car parking spaces beneath it; crucially, a two-tier shopping street
could flank the raised park and provide an overlapping solution to the level changes, which would
also provide the space for the number of shops required. It was a bold move, not least because
the design team was determined not to build anything mall-like, something project director Rod
Holmes was incredibly anxious about at the time. But the idea, which has since metamorphosed
into the slightly realigned South John Street, worked. Locating anchor stores at either end of this
double-level thoroughfare (one opening onto Lord Street, the other onto Canning Place) created
part of a much-needed pedestrian circuit. The retention of other streets, Paradise and Hanover
Streets in particular, ensured that the development remained inextricably linked to the rest of the
city while adding to the range of scale within the project. If South John Street had something of
the busy two-level street about it, then Paradise Street could be more of a boulevard – indeed, it

could even accommodate a tram system that was being promoted by Merseytravel at the time. (The rebuilt Paradise Street was, in fact, constructed to accommodate a tram system, but the project was controversially cancelled in 2004 after running into funding problems with central government.)

Significantly, the decision was also taken very early on in the concept phases of the project to divide the development into distinct 'urban districts' and to share the work between a large number of different design firms. Carefully crafting the scale of this development was always important to Grosvenor, which was adamant that it would not build a 'monolithic' scheme. It would have been relatively simple, in the name of consistency, to employ a single approach in terms of scale, materiality and detailing – but Grosvenor judged that successful cities are just not characterised in that manner. Even the most rigidly planned environments become fragmented and take on their own small-scale personalities, while people expect some variety in their surroundings: boulevards and alleyways; broad vistas and pocket parks; prominent buildings and quieter places which await discovery. The proposal was to create 'a tapestry of small and large buildings and spaces' within the site. Variety not uniformity. As the masterplan developed, this idea of 'urban districts' became absolutely fundamental to everything Grosvenor did. Consequently, the Paradise Street Development Area came to be thought of as five distinct, but overlapping, districts:

- Paradise Street: a cosmopolitan, pedestrian boulevard of some grandeur flanked by 'city scale' buildings leading to the 'architectural statement' of an anchor store. Double-height shop frontages and residential units.
- Hanover Street: a busy and eclectic street, open to traffic, creating an interface between the rest of the scheme and the bars and former warehouses of the Rope Walks.

'The fundamental approach is to treat the Paradise Street Development Area as a series of related development opportunities, fully integrated with the existing city centre'

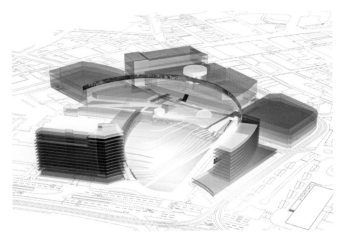
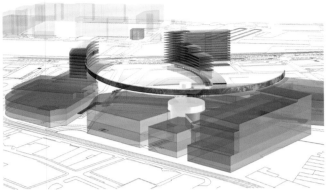

- Peter's Lane: small-scale, partially covered streets, preserving historic buildings and responding to the proximity of the Grade 1 listed Bluecoat Arts Centre, a much-loved building within the heart of Liverpool.
- South John Street: a two-tier, partially covered, galleried shopping street that links the two anchor department stores. Protection from the weather without being fully enclosed.
- The Pool and Park: this is the development's grand gesture – a park, dramatically tiered, framed by bars and restaurants, with views across the site of the city's original pool towards the Albert Dock and the Mersey.

'The fundamental approach is to treat the Paradise Street Development Area as a series of related development opportunities, fully integrated with the existing city centre,' stated Grosvenor's brief to architects. 'The masterplan creates several new places, not one large development, and provides

The reason that Liverpool One feels so natural is that every thought process, each twist and turn of the designer's pen, was tested to within an inch of its life

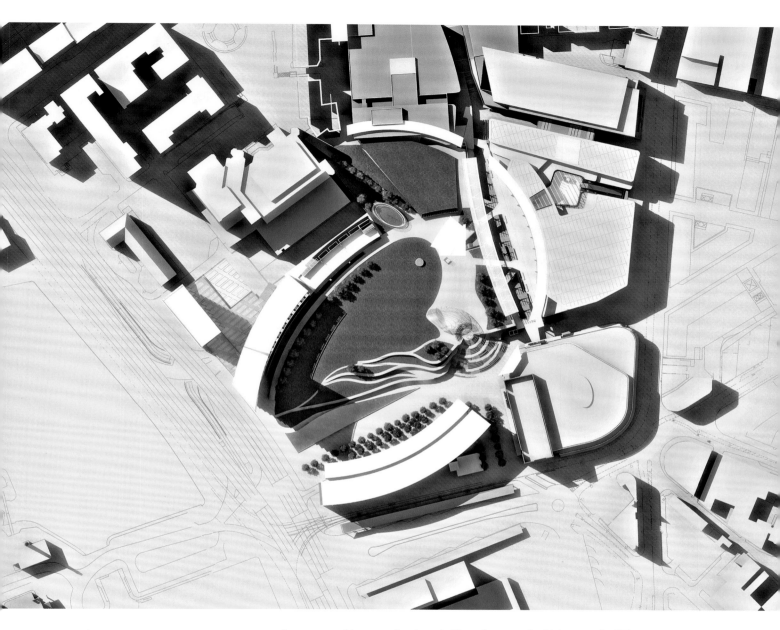

scope for a new architecture that is varied but always to the highest quality.' The consequence of adopting such a position was that Grosvenor, which was eventually to recruit 26 architecture practices to each design a component of the project, had to perform a precarious balancing act. The search for variety could not result in an architectural zoo, while participating architects had to be given a certain amount of creative freedom – otherwise, why commission them at all? Also, the variety that was so fundamental to the development must not look too contrived. Grosvenor and masterplanners BDP clearly had their work cut out here, drawing up guidelines for development without writing a rule book.

this page
View towards the park, with the waterfront beyond. The buildings here are deliberately grand, echoing the strength and robustness of Liverpool's historic structures. They are also rather rounded, like dockside steps.

right
The surface detailing of Thomas
Steers Way marks the edge of
Liverpool's original wet dock.

Today, the completed development appears inherently logical. It's as if the masterplan couldn't be drawn any other way. It didn't seem like that at the beginning, however, and the reason that Liverpool One feels so natural now is that every thought process, each twist and turn of the designer's pen, was tested to within an inch of its life. Nothing was left unchallenged and every permutation was scrutinised by a review panel chaired by Rod Holmes, who assumed the role of design champion by ensuring that Grosvenor's insistence on high quality was never forgotten. It is also important to note that there was never just a single over-arching idea that drove the project onward; rather, there were dozens of agendas, pressures, constraints, demands, wish-lists, visions, flashes of inspiration and other criteria which all got poured into the designer's mix. One point of departure was plotting the locations of all listed buildings and other structures of architectural or historic merit, something that certainly helped influence the design team's approach to scale, materials and conservation matters, especially for the zone east of Paradise Street. Maximising connectivity was another influence, creating not only a seamless extension of Liverpool's shopping area but also providing quick, direct and intuitive links with the city's other districts – the business zone, the waterfront and the Rope Walks. Pedestrian movement further influenced the project, and the team took into account walking times and 'desire lines', affording clear views through the development from a wide variety of angles. Materials were also considered at an early stage of the project. The masterplanning team went to considerable lengths to map out the facade treatments of different buildings throughout the site, negotiating a careful response to the predominantly stone-clad buildings of Church and Lord Streets to the north of the development, and the brick at the south-eastern edges. The whole approach was one of incremental, iterative advances – so much

THE 'URBAN RENAISSANCE'

so that there were very few 'Eureka!' moments. Both Grosvenor and BDP agree that the design process was 'truly a collaborative effort'.

It is actually remarkable how much of the original masterplan drafts is discernible in the finished project: the location of the anchor stores; the two-tiered South John Street; the re-routing of Manesty's Lane as part of a 'discovery axis' linking the Bluecoat Chambers to the Albert Dock; the curved facade of the southern department store (now John Lewis) to echo the curves of the other buildings which converge on that site; the public spaces which trace the lines of the original dock; the creation of a new link with Church Street by punching through a building to establish the Peter's Lane arcade; the five distinct districts ... all of which are clearly identifiable in Liverpool One. 'The masterplan is still very recognisable as that developed in 2000, with each succeeding architect adding further richness, variety and detail,' wrote BDP architects Terry Davenport and Richard Rees in *Urban Design* magazine.

Other aspects of the scheme were not so quickly resolved. The location of the bus station was one issue which proved a difficult nut to crack, largely due to long and difficult discussions with the

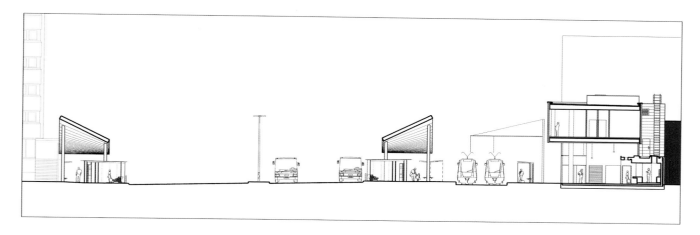

above
Section through Canning Place,
illustrating the bus station and
(on the right) the travel information
centre embedded within what was
to become the Hilton hotel.

local transport authority. The planning submissions of 2001 (one in January, followed by a revised scheme the following October taking account of objections) locate the bus station not in Canning Place, where it was eventually built, but adjacent to the park. At the time, nobody was convinced this was the best place for the buses, and the government-run Commission for Architecture and the Built Environment was especially uncertain. Nonetheless, a planning submission was made on the understanding that the location of the bus station was a moot point, and it wasn't finally manoeuvred into Canning Place until 2004.

As it has turned out, the five districts aren't quite as distinctive as originally envisaged (even a 42 acre site is probably too small for dramatic fluctuations of style and character), while the final form of Chavasse Park and the way it meets South John Street proved to be a particularly thorny issue to resolve. Eventually, in 2003, Grosvenor invited Cesar Pelli, Rafael Viñoly and Terry Farrell (all three, architects of 'iconic' international standing) to comment on the park problem. Pelli's

'The masterplan is still very recognisable as that developed in 2000, with each succeeding architect adding further richness, variety and detail'

previous page
With three levels of shops and restaurants, South John Street is an almost Piranesian stretch of bridges, arcades and walkways. It is a dramatic cut through the city centre, a common-sense solution to the topography of central Liverpool.

practice, Pelli Clarke Pelli Architects, was appointed on the basis of its concept of 'an ellipse against the sky', a pair of dramatic arcs that sculpt their way through the development. These arresting curves manage to provide a sense of integration to the park and surrounding buildings, rather than leaving them as a set of adjacencies. South John Street, the Hilton hotel and a residential block all become pieces within a larger composition, and even a corner of the John Lewis department store gets shaved off as the architect's compass sweeps across the site. Pelli's vision was also an attempt to stitch the wider city together, mediating between the tighter urban grain of the Rope Walks and the more expansive commercial district. 'Basically, it was genius. It was two lines on a plan,' says John Bullough.

Rod Holmes liked it too. 'I think it's rather wonderful,' he told one of the regular design meetings with the city council. In fact, that design continued to evolve and the final resolution of the park did not emerge until rather late in the day – high level access, for example, was once to be gained through a series of ramps, a design tactic that has since been replaced with a flight of monolithic steps which ripple out of the park as a faint echo of those curves which race across the masterplan. The gradient of the park also altered over time, as did the design and location of the sculptural pavilions which populate it. That is the nature of design; nothing pops out of the designer's mind fully formed, and certainly the competing pressures of this gargantuan scheme meant that every 'solution' was the subject of an almost endless process of refinement. And the trouble with that is that a change here very often forces an alteration there. Underlying the entire project, though, is that idea of connectivity, the motivation to use the site both as a centre of gravity (drawing people in) and as a hub (sending them back out). 'We wanted a high degree of permeability,' says Bill Butler, partner at Pelli Clarke Pelli Architects. 'We wanted comfortable, natural and meaningful pedestrian flow. That was something we spent an incredible amount of time working on.'

And local people are tremendously grateful for that. 'What I find particularly interesting, as someone who was born and bred in Liverpool, is the changes to the topography to the city. It joins the dots. From the business district we can now walk to places in 10 minutes when we once had to take a cab. And it's a pleasant walk,' says Chamber of Commerce leader Jack Stopforth.

this page
South John Street. Partially protected
by a canopy, this multi-layered street
is open enough to avoid becoming
too mall-like. It is a bustling place –
vibrant, colourful and well connected
to the adjacent park.

THE 'URBAN RENAISSANCE'

Chapter 3
CONSENT

Chapter 3
CONSENT

previous page
The car park, at the south-west corner of the site, designed by Wilkinson Eyre. This was one of a handful of buildings which began operating prior to the two big openings in 2008.

left
Signing up anchor stores, like John Lewis, was crucial to the planning process. Compulsory Purchase Orders (CPOs) were used to acquire land, and it was important to demonstrate that the entire project was a realistic commercial proposition.

It was never going to be easy

To the passer-by, gazing through hoardings at the muscular business of construction, the sharp end of regeneration is a matter of digging through earth, of pouring concrete. Indeed, people often wonder why it has taken so long for the builders to get on with the job, and it is a common source of local anxiety and frustration that a development site can lie untouched long after the vision for it has been unveiled. The answer rests in the planning of it all – in the near endless technical discussions, consultations, permissions and legal agreements that have to be thrashed out (often through public inquiries) before a single sod can be turned. This, truly, is where the action is. It is a behind-the-scenes business, one of heading off challenges before they arise, and dealing with them when they do. In Liverpool, where 275 interests occupied space across 42 acres of city centre real estate, securing planning permission was only part of the battle; acquiring the land was arguably the bigger struggle.

One of Grosvenor's inspired moves was the appointment of Giulia Bunting, from planning consultants Drivers Jonas, as part of the team at the very beginning. Grosvenor's John Bullough, who led the Liverpool project during its crucial early stages, had once been on the opposing side to Bunting in a compulsory purchase inquiry and he made sure they were on the same side this time. The appointment also strengthened Grosvenor's hand at the selection stage because Bunting's presence was a strong signal that a serious response to planning issues would inform

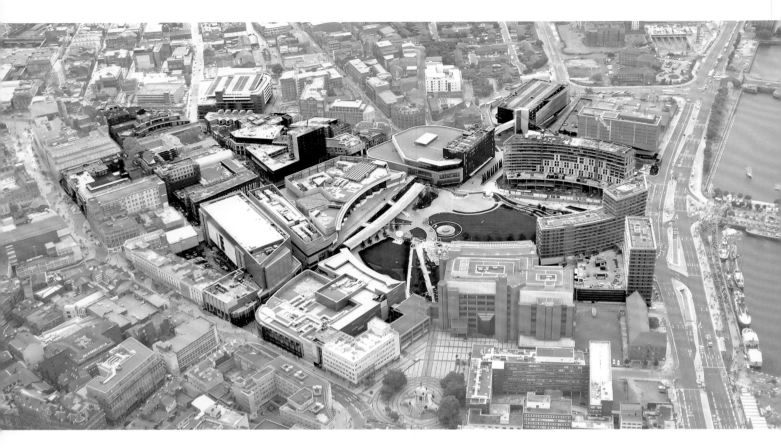

above
The condition of the project in August 2008. The majority of the buildings have been completed and South John Street has opened for business.

opposite
Liverpool One borders a World Heritage Site and a conservation area. The masterplanning team, and the planning consultants in particular, had to be careful that building designs were sympathetic to their surroundings while remaining contemporary demonstrations of renewal.

the development of the scheme at the very highest level, rather than become retrofitted when events dictated it. As far as anyone can remember, Grosvenor was the only shortlisted developer which included a planner on the presentation team. So far, Liverpool One is the most complex scheme Bunting has ever worked on.

Some of the complexities are obvious. Although the city council owned one third of the land that had been earmarked for development (and was prepared to lease it to Grosvenor), the rest had to be assembled by merely making someone an offer, or pursuing compulsory purchase orders. One of the landowners fought particularly hard, and continued to object even after a public inquiry had found in Grosvenor's favour. Also, Grosvenor had taken the decision to commission more than 20 architects to work on different plots throughout the site, making planning submissions and public consultation far more cumbersome than if a single design firm had been involved. Furthermore, the development was not limited to buildings – there were roads (and road closures), provision for a tram system, the demolition and replacement of a fire station, public spaces ... It was always going to be a long, hard slog.

Other complexities were less obvious, however, and potentially far more worrying. One problem was that a rival developer, the Walton Group, had a claim on Chavasse Park and intended to build a large shopping mall on it – a plan that was incompatible with Grosvenor's intentions and a far cry from what the city council was prepared to entertain. And it didn't help that the city's

this page
Debenhams, too, was an important
signing. Debenhams and John Lewis
sit at either end of South John Street,
'anchoring' the development in
retail terms.

Consultation

Throughout the development of Liverpool One, Grosvenor took consultation seriously. They had to; part of the reason the developer had been commissioned in the first place was its commitment to partnership. Stephen Musgrave, who had become chief executive of Grosvenor Great Britain & Ireland at the time of the appointment, remembers giving Liverpool city officials a very honest appraisal of the challenge: 'We said to the council "We're not coming in here telling you how we're going to develop the city, because we don't know. And we're not giving you all the answers, because we don't know them".'

Consultation extended far beyond the national agencies which are legally entitled to a hearing, such as English Heritage and the Commission for Architecture and the Built Environment. Small local groups were also included in discussions, while public meetings were a strong feature of the development process. Indeed, special interest groups and members of the public who responded to press notices helped consolidate the form of the emerging masterplan at a series of workshops held between September and December 2000. The masterplan that was submitted for planning in January 2001 was resubmitted the following October after an extensive consultation exercise. Between January 2001 and September 2002 the city council received just 67 formal responses from consultation initiatives. 'The lack of significant objection to the planning application was in my view remarkable having regard to the scale and complexity of the proposals,' Michael Burchnall, from the city council's planning department, told a public inquiry.

A scale model of part of the development area was put on display at a four-day public exhibition in May 2001. The full Paradise Project model went on permanent display on 17 November 2004 when Grosvenor opened the Liverpool One Information Centre on Lord Street, a stone's throw from the development itself.

'What Grosvenor, and Rod Holmes in particular, did absolutely brilliantly was the engagement with the stakeholders,' said Giulia Bunting, of planning consultants Drivers Jonas.

'Holmes's willingness to join in Liverpool's blossoming business scene, speaking about the the project to various audiences with charm and dry humour, has made him a minor celebrity in the city,' wrote Paul Unger in *Property Week*. 'Every 12 weeks Holmes and his right-hand man, technical director Bill Allen, take over a city centre cinema to update both the public and business communities on progress. The information centre on Lord Street is the scene of a constant stream of fluorescent-bibbed visitors off on a site tour.'

Apart from landowners and occupiers, and the regular workshops held with the city council's Members' Working Group, Grosvenor consulted dozens of organisations, from the Ancient Monuments Society and the city's fire service to cycle campaigners and residents' associations. The full list of consultees can be found in Appendix C.

Unitary Development Plan (UDP), which had been in the making since the early 1990s and was close to completion, made little or no mention of the site or the Paradise Street project. A UDP is an important document, one that takes many years to put together, setting out a local authority's planning priorities and broad intentions. 'Ideally, you want a clear policy and an up-to-date plan. What we had was a Unitary Development Plan that covered the whole of Liverpool but which was almost completely silent on this,' says Bunting. The council had, however, compiled a document called the Paradise Street Development Framework which was drawn up to be read in parallel to its emerging UDP, but this hardly gave it the same legal status.

Liverpool City Council was a nervous client. Too many high-profile projects had come to nothing, and officials were absolutely determined that the extension to the city's main retail area, encompassing Paradise Street and its environs, would happen along the lines that Grosvenor proposed. Risk had to be minimised wherever possible. Just about everyone involved was new to projects of this ambition and scale, so a slow, steady advance was far more preferable to a rapid dash forward. 'You have to understand, most local authorities do this kind of thing once in every lifetime,' explained Bunting. 'The whole climate of the planning phase was that we couldn't do anything that could possibly be challenged. We had to be whiter than white.'

The path to planning permission

Once Grosvenor, with its funding partner Henderson, had been appointed by Liverpool City Council, the rush was on to complete the masterplan and submit a planning application. The hope was that an outline plan would be ready by October 2000, but the sheer complexity of the project pushed an application back by three months. On 16 January 2001 Giulia Bunting, on behalf of Grosvenor/Henderson, completed the city council's standard tick-box planning application and wrote a cheque covering the application fee of £21,470. In a covering letter she made the point that

this page
South John Street, an open, multi-layered, pedestrian zone. The fact that the development was not a mall worked in Grosvenor's favour during a public inquiry into modifications to the city council's Unitary Development Plan (UDP).

Significantly, very few land
owners and occupiers objected
to Grosvenor's plans on principle
– many wanted the scheme to
progress, but requested that their
premises be left alone. Exceptions
could not be made, however. The
success of the project depended
on its being 'comprehensive'.

the plans were not being presented as a *fait accompli*. They were, rather, an expression of intent, a platform from which detail could evolve. 'The PSDA is seen as a high-priority project which should be brought forward at the earliest possible date. However it is a complex project and one which will continue to develop through time. The approach to the planning submission has been tailored to enable the proposals to be brought forward into the formal planning arena as soon as practically possible, but with scope for them to continue to evolve,' she wrote. 'It is Grosvenor/Henderson's intention to seek an outline planning permission for the entire development, in order to establish the principles for the development of the whole of the PSDA and to provide the framework within which to proceed to the next stage of design development.'

It was an unusual application because it was something of a hybrid. Typically, proposals of this scale are approved in two stages: there is an outline phase to establish the principles of a proposal,

where matters such as the broad outlines, sizes and positions of buildings are defined; detail follows later. But part of the development zone contained listed buildings and fell inside a conservation area, and the Grosvenor team was acutely aware that World Heritage Site status was becoming more and more likely, so the decision was taken to lodge an outline planning application which also contained detailed plans for specific plots around the historic Bluecoat Arts Centre. It was a smart idea (relatively unusual then, but more common today), but it would still be nearly two years before planning consent was granted.

The planning application was, in fact, resubmitted in October 2001 to take account of comments and critiques emerging from a wide-ranging consultation exercise – involving national agencies such as English Heritage and the Commission for Architecture and the Built Environment right down to smaller, local groups including Merseytravel, the Merseyside Civic Society and the

Merseyside Archaeological Service. Tenants and landowners were also canvassed for their opinions, and the resubmitted masterplan provided for 23 revisions. Importantly, the principles and broad tactical moves underpinning the masterplan remained unchanged, and a comparison of both 2001 plans reveals few obvious amendments.

While the design was undergoing its slow evolution, Grosvenor and Liverpool's planning team was becoming increasingly anxious about that matter of the Unitary Development Plan. It was clear that compulsory purchase would be needed to assemble the site, and the best way to ensure a successful outcome would be to amend the UDP to take account of the city council's ambitions for what was then the Paradise Street Development Area. It would also help in settling the dispute with the Walton Group, and would minimise the danger of having the entire scheme 'called in' and scrutinised at national level by the Secretary of State with responsibility for the environment. The trouble was, such a major amendment to the UDP would require a public inquiry – effectively delaying the project for a year. The team opted for caution, believing that the delay would eventually lead to more certainty, and probably time saved later on. The public inquiry ran from November 2001 to February 2002. Healey & Baker's Mark McVicar, acting for the local authority, issued a strong and unambiguous statement to the inquiry: 'A comprehensive development solution for

below

Liverpool One contains few covered spaces. A public inquiry concluded in 2002 that open spaces were 'infinitely preferable' to a self-contained shopping mall.

below right

The Lord Street end of South John Street. This large building is composed of interlocking blocks, each defined by its own material, in an effort to reduce its bulk.

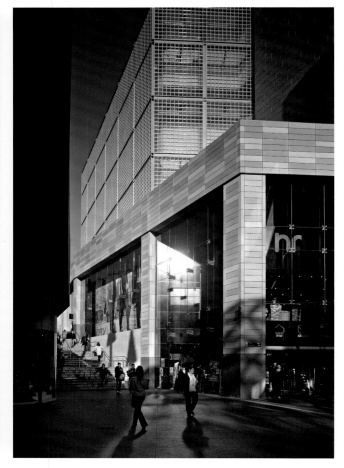

the Paradise Street Development Area is necessary to ensure the desired integration of disparate quarters of the city centre, to secure regeneration of derelict buildings of architectural merit and long-standing under-utilised land; to provide a diversified and sustainable improvement to the city centre offer as a whole; and secure the long-term role, vitality and viability of Liverpool city centre as a centre of regional importance.' McVicar also added that a scheme along the lines proposed by Grosvenor would provide 'a catalyst for the necessary step change in the future prospects of Liverpool city centre'.

It worked. In May 2002 Richard Mordey, the inspector chairing the public inquiry, published a report accepting the city council's case for modifying the UDP. 'Duke wins fight for heart of city' announced the *Liverpool Echo*. Mordey's verdict was clear: 'The Paradise Street Development Area represents a unique opportunity to bring vacant sites and buildings back into use, to improve and reuse buildings of historic interest, providing attractive linkages to the main retail area, the Rope Walks, Chavasse Park and on the Waterfront. This approach is infinitely preferable to a self-contained, mall-based design.' Mordey formally dismissed the Walton Group's challenge a few weeks later, a decision backed by the Secretary of State, who then added to the sense of relief on 22 October by issuing a letter to confirm that the scheme would not be called in. Suddenly, the entire project had an air of certainty about it and momentum quickly picked up. The council

left

The car park at the south-west of the site. This part of the masterplan proved to be the most difficult to resolve. Although the original planning application was made in January 2001, it took until February 2004 to draw up an outline planning application which dealt with this area successfully.

right

Grosvenor's planning submission was relatively unusual. Drawn up as a hybrid application, it asked for broad outline consent for the entire development, while including detailed designs for a variety of buildings around the Bluecoat Arts Centre.

adopted the revised Unitary Development Plan in November. On 19 December Grosvenor and Liverpool City Council finally signed the Development Agreement and agreed the terms of 'Section 106' works (covering matters like respect for the archaeology, phasing, highway improvements and provision for maintenance). On 23 December 2002 planning permission was granted.

Compulsory purchase

Many sitting tenants, however, could see where it was all going and the owners of Quiggins vowed to fight the development before it was even granted planning permission. Quiggins, something of a Liverpool institution, was a multi-tenanted building which offered an independent, alternative shopping experience: antiques, second-hand clothes, tattoos and the like. Theirs was by far the loudest voice of protest, although the Society of Friends protested too. It was clear that some sites earmarked for development would have to be purchased compulsorily, a process that would involve a second public inquiry. At the time it seemed to the Grosvenor team that the goalposts were continually being moved – no sooner was one hurdle overcome than another would appear in view. 'I just could not rest until I knew for certain that we were beyond legal challenge,' said Rod Holmes. Having to resort to compulsory purchase also caused Grosvenor to pursue potential occupiers of the new development with renewed vigour. It was particularly important to sign up the large 'anchor' stores to prove that the scheme was a realistic commercial proposition. 'You can't just take someone's land unless you can show that you have a viable scheme. John Lewis and Debenhams signing up was absolutely crucial,' says Bunting.

The city council promoted compulsory purchase orders (CPOs) in March 2003, and there were relatively few objections. In fact, only 15 people who were affected by the CPOs had even bothered to comment on the masterplan during the highly publicised public consultation events over the previous couple of years. Some objected, or postured, simply to strengthen their negotiating power; only one or two really meant it. In all, the city council received 56 objections from a wide

above
Formerly the Eagle pub, this historic building is now home to a Sony store. Prior to becoming a pub, however, the building was a US consulate, facing the dock designed by Thomas Steers.

above
Mixed-use building on Paradise Street, containing shops, apartments and a crèche.

range of organisations including the BBC, the Merseyside Fire Service, Lloyds TSB, the Ramblers' Association and even the Government Office for the North West. The majority, however, were merely seeking clarifications and reassurances, including the local diocese which wanted nothing more than a confirmation that a local memorial garden would be treated with respect. By the time the public inquiry began, 44 objections had been withdrawn.

Grosvenor's Guy Butler says that objections were specific, rather than principled: 'No one stood up and said they didn't want the scheme to happen ... they all sympathised with the Paradise Project. But the objectors just asked if they could be left out of it.' This was the main problem – too many people were asking why their little parcel of land made such a difference to the success of such a vast development. Each hoped that an exception could be made for their specific plot without damaging the integrity of the project. Grosvenor and the city council had to hold their nerve and grant no special favours.

'A number of objectors argue that minor modifications could avoid the need to acquire their property,' wrote Peter Drummond, chief executive of masterplanners BDP, in his submission

The view from English Heritage

It stands to reason, believes Henry Owen-John, the North-West's regional director for conservation body English Heritage, that early consultation over large regeneration projects will have nothing but long term benefits. It engenders trust; it establishes support for underlying principles; and it sets the tone for working relationships that may well be sorely tested during the life of complex and drawn-out developments. 'However, this was not widely understood in 1999. But Grosvenor did understand it, and I think this is to their credit,' he says.

Owen-John was in close contact with Grosvenor's development team throughout most of the life of the Liverpool One project, although his involvement tailed off as approved designs began to be built (and a key member of his staff went to work directly for the city council). Preying on his mind was the fact that this was the largest single building programme in Liverpool for 100 years. The strength of the city's industrial archaeology, the World Heritage Site listing (secured in 2004), the presence of listed buildings and a conservation zone all gave Owen-John a statutory right to be consulted. But he recalls consultation being significant, genuine and constructive rather than perfunctory.

The process was also eased by the quality of the masterplan. Owen-John instantly approved of the efforts to create something distinctly Liverpudlian. And in spite of the diversity of the architectural programme, he detected a certain coherence at the outset. 'It was a really good concept,' he says.

So good, in fact, that English Heritage had only one serious objection to the entire project – the height and massing of Cesar Pelli's One Park West building, which became a serious stumbling block (see pages 178–87). 'For something of this magnitude I think it's pretty remarkable that we had only one major issue. There was robust talking, but we worked our way through it,' he remembers. 'One of the crucial things was that, where we had a distinctly different position, we were able to sit down at a table and talk it through. That "can-do" attitude was good.'

right

Elevation of the Liver Street car park,
with a section through the footbridge
over to John Lewis. The building
in the background lies outside the
Liverpool One area.

right

Elevation of key Paradise Street
buildings, east side. The buildings
gradually increase in scale from the
original structures to the left. School
Lane and College Lane are preserved
as small-scale routes running off this
grand boulevard.

right

Here, the new elevation of School
Lane is revealed. Historic buildings
(including the Bluecoat, and the
County Palatine and Russell buildings)
are preserved and framed by new
additions. The arcade designed by
Dixon Jones architects is located
centre-right.

above

Section through the development,
illustrating how the design team has
responded to the changing scale
of the context – large and entirely
new on the left, smaller and more
contextual towards the right.

to the second public inquiry. 'The cumulative impact, however, of these objections and subsequent minor modifications would compromise the overall design of the masterplan and the comprehensive renewal of Liverpool city centre. In response to all the objections I am minded to stress the importance of the PSDA masterplan's approach in developing this area comprehensively.'

The word 'comprehensive' was a common feature of submissions to the inquiry, which ran from November 2003 to January 2004. The driving idea was that a single developer should develop the entire site all at once. It was certainly not to be a piecemeal exercise. 'The principal stakeholders agree that the "step change" that is needed in the performance of the city centre requires *comprehensive* regeneration,' Rod Holmes told the inquiry. 'The changes simply will not occur unless they are masterplanned and delivered comprehensively.' Michael Burchnall, one of the city council's planning chiefs, made a particularly hard-hitting plea: 'I believe that the

right
The Zig Zag stair and escalator
running deep into the central retail-
leisure block on Paradise Street,
west. Locating such a deep cut
into the building at this point was
deliberate – it would provide a
view of the Liver Building from
College Lane.

opposite
This image shows the work of
three architectural practices.
Twenty-six practices worked on
the development, but all planning
applications were channelled through
consultants Drivers Jonas. These
consultants acted as the 'post box'.

above
The Debenhams department store acts as the gateway building at the northern end of South John Street. This portion of the Liverpool One project opened on 29 May 2008.

Jim Gill, chief executive, Liverpool Vision

When I joined Liverpool Vision in the summer of 2001 the city council had already appointed Grosvenor as its development partner for the Paradise Street Development Area. Our chairman, Sir Joe Dwyer, had participated in the selection process and told me how his advice had focused on the strength of Grosvenor as a long-term partner, which he felt was the key factor. How right he was! I have witnessed, and occasionally been party to, the early tensions as a partnership deal was hammered out on terms to suit both parties, and the more or less exemplary way in which Grosvenor has gone about the masterplanning, detailed design and construction management of the project.

Liverpudlians had seen lots of grand ideas over the years, but little in the way of real delivery. This was different. The Grosvenor team invested time, money and dogged single-mindedness in achieving understanding and acceptance of its plans; they made sure they got through a series of public workshops which set new standards in public engagement. There were times when the strain on individuals and on partner relationships was clearly visible, but the investment in securing wider public support and the confidence in Grosvenor's ability to deliver was a major factor in pulling the scheme through.

With Liverpool One, Grosvenor has invested in the long-term future of Liverpool. This developer has constantly reminded us of the importance of careful and thorough preparation and the value that arises from quality design and delivery. Grosvenor has delivered on its commitments to the thousands of people who invested time and confidence in the process that shaped Liverpool One.

comprehensive scheme is fundamental to the further regeneration of Liverpool city centre and that it is in the national and public interest that the scheme is implemented and completed as soon as possible.'

Again, the inspector found in Grosvenor's and the city council's favour, and the small handful of die-hards who pursued their cases right the way through the inquiry were forced to sell or at least cooperate. It was, inevitably, to prove an expensive exercise and the land purchases amounted to around £180 million – the largest payment went to the HSBC pension fund and the smallest to a palm reader. Quiggins, in spite of Grosvenor's efforts to tempt them with alternative accommodation nearby, continued to fight and even threatened High Court action to appeal against the CPO decision. But they finally dropped any objection allowing work to begin on the eastern side in 2006. The whole city breathed a sigh of relief, not least because the intention was to complete the development during 2008 when the eyes of Europe would be on Liverpool as the EU's Capital of Culture. 'Now, thanks to the pragmatism of Quiggins, it looks more likely that this will be an achievable goal,' said an editorial in the *Liverpool Daily Post*. 'Now it is of vital importance that the Grosvenor development runs as smoothly as possible. The development is a sign that the city is preparing to change, grow and develop.'

By the end of 2004 everything, including funding, was in place. On 22 November the Duke of Westminster and council leader Mike Storey climbed into a digger and scooped out the first symbolic bucketful of soil.

below
Hanover Street. Grosvenor
rehabilitated more elderly
buildings than it needed to –
certainly more than were protected
by a historic listing. Here, facades
are protected while remedial work
takes place inside.

Process

By the time the diggers finally moved in, the masterplan had undergone a final set of tweaks
and amendments, resulting in an entirely new planning application on 27 February 2004. It was
this application, approved on 9 July, that settled once and for all the precise location of the bus
station. This had always been a moot point, partly because of uncertainty over the introduction
of a tram system to the city. The revised masterplan also included minor changes to the 'red line'
boundary at the south-west corner of the site, finally establishing what was inside and outside of the
development zone. However, it was still much the same hybrid application that had been submitted
in 2001, although the masterplan kept open a set of alternatives regarding the location of luxury
apartments and a five star hotel. But converting the outline consent into detailed consent, apart
from the five plots mentioned above, had yet to be done. This proved to be yet another hurdle.

Because the city council had wanted as much clarity and certainty as possible, Grosvenor's outline
applications (the one lodged and revised in 2001 and the final version of February 2004) had been
very specific about elements such as building outline, boundaries and access points. Ideally, the
architects chosen to develop the individual plots into detailed proposals would have worked entirely
within the outlines set out by masterplanners BDP; overlaying the detail could have been dealt with
under what are known as 'reserved matters'. However, changes began to emerge to a number of
buildings within the scheme, some driven by tenants, including adjustments to the line of a building
or the position of principal entrances. This meant making entirely new planning applications.

In fact, 75 per cent of the 34 plots throughout the development had to be resubmitted as fresh planning applications. Grosvenor and Drivers Jonas began to regret being so specific so early, especially as the project was always going to evolve incrementally over a number of years. However, the planning system then made it more difficult to introduce the necessary flexibility and the city council required certainty on a number of matters. In retrospect, says Bunting, it might have been worth giving the design team more room for manoeuvre by identifying the footprint of each building but locating it a little less precisely within its plot. That way alterations to building line and shape would have been accommodated far more easily.

Liverpool One proceeded very much along the lines of the Empire State Building in 1930, in that construction work was under way before all the detailed design had been completed. This certainly added a sense of urgency to the project, and efficiency was paramount. Matters were simplified somewhat by making Drivers Jonas the single point of contact for planning submissions. The company was, effectively, the project's post box. Rather than subject the city council to the paperwork of 26 architectural practices, Julia Chowings (who worked with Bunting) acted as a conduit, delivering all new planning applications and revisions to a single format. The status of every single application (whether pending, under consideration or approved) was tracked and administered by Chowings. Everybody knew what had to happen, and when. 'We were the post box. Everything came from us and went through our door,' says Chowings. Surprises were kept to a minimum. The city council reciprocated by putting dedicated planning staff on the job and delegating the planning decisions to a specialist working party – only three sites had to be approved by the planning committee, including Cesar Pelli's landmark tower. The cooperation and consistency shown by the city council's planning team, which worked closely with Drivers Jonas throughout the history of the development, were key to the success of the project. The fact that Liverpool was to take the Capital of Culture title in 2008 began to weigh on people's minds; in spite of the determination to achieve something of spectacularly high quality, everyone concerned had to press that little bit harder if the city was to be more than a construction site when it was most in the public eye.

right
Cesar Pelli's One Park West under construction. English Heritage objected to the proposed height of this building, and it was reduced by three storeys. Fighting the heritage lobby could well have ended in a third public inquiry.

Chapter 4
RETAIL STRATEGY

Chapter 4
RETAIL STRATEGY

The retail mix

In just a single morning, on 29 May 2008, Liverpool's newly opened John Lewis store sold 10 £1,000 coffee machines. The old store on nearby Church Street stocked these luxury items, but never sold any. The date is significant – this was the day that the first phase of Liverpool One opened and, to the thud of dramatic music and a dance spectacular, crowds of waiting people poured into South John Street to explore what had been rising behind the hoardings. The coffee machine anecdote illustrates two things: first, that high-quality spaces will encourage people to spend money they wouldn't otherwise part with; and, second, that the new development really would encourage affluent consumers from Liverpool's suburbs and outer fringes to shop in the city centre. By lunchtime on the opening day, it already appeared that Grosvenor's mighty but calculated gamble had been worth taking.

There are, of course, more reliable figures than the sale of coffee machines which underpin the health of Liverpool One. In the first three weeks of trading, John Lewis's turnover increased by around 50 per cent; two months later pedestrian flows along Church Street were consistently 30–40 per cent higher than they had been previously, and even the Metquarter, a high-quality shopping mall nearby, was witnessing a similar increase in the number of shoppers. This is all highly significant because Liverpool One was never meant to compete with the city's original shopping centre – it was meant, instead, to extend the 'main retail area' and create sufficient critical mass to draw people back

right

This early sketch shows that masterplanners originally intended Liverpool One to contain three anchor stores (see red dots), creating a retail triangle. The third anchor on the right did not materialise, however, and the masterplanning team split the building in two to accommodate a pair of large tenants, rather than a single retail giant.

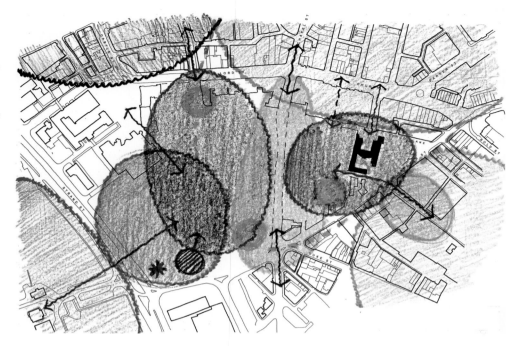

into the city. Occasionally, the way in which this integration works is counter-intuitive. The local fashion retailer Peacocks, for example, has seen sales in its original store increase even though it opened a second shop in Liverpool One. Music outlet HMV and fashion store New Look have also opened units in the new development without closing their original stores elsewhere in the city and without any drop in revenue. What Liverpool One seems to have done is redefine the city and pull people in. 'This is regeneration. Bringing more people into the city is regeneration,' says Jenefer Greenwood, Grosvenor's retail strategist.

Retail strategy has evolved over the last three or four decades to encompass a handful of key principles, most of which have been expressed in covered shopping malls. There are two principal configurations: the classic dumb-bell, in which a strip of shops is flanked by two anchors (such as Cribbs Causeway, near Bristol); and the triangle, in which three large anchor stores form the corners with smaller and more speciality shops in-between (pioneered by Bluewater, outside London in Kent). The anchor stores are required to provide the quality assurance, big brands and the range of products that will attract people to the development – without them, no development will be viable. Equally, the mid-size and smaller units are necessary to offer a more complete shopping experience. It is this thinking that lies at the heart of Liverpool One, even though the development is a more integrated urban environment than a covered mall. Originally, the development was predicated around the idea of three anchor stores, one at either end of South John Street and a third located in the maze of lanes behind the Bluecoat Arts Centre, but a market emerged for this third store from large rather than vast retailers, and the building was divided in two. Jenefer Greenwood says retail developments should also be characterised by 'width and depth'; not only should all tastes and budgets be catered for, but competition between shops in the same class should also be introduced. The system has more logic to it than is immediately obvious. As well as catering for particular budgets, modern retail developments have to respond to spending habits that mix luxury items with low-cost goods – people across all social strata might well add a

right
Marks & Spencer, a long-established presence on the UK High Street, has a store just outside Liverpool One on Church Street. In a sense, M&S represents the 'third anchor' for the development.

Gucci or Tiffany sparkle to an outfit by Primark. Shops can no longer differentiate themselves along demographic lines. This seems to be especially true of Liverpool which, according to retailers, is particularly brand aware, while the Grand National and May Chester races give local fashion stores unseasonal boosts that are rare elsewhere in the UK. Furthermore, retail developers are having to get to grips with what fashion magazines term 'aspirational' brands, a sort of upper-middle range

Retail strategy has evolved over recent decades to encompass a handful of key principles, most of which have been expressed in covered shopping malls

right
Half of all the retailers attracted
to the development are new to
Liverpool. Signing Apple, though,
was a coup for the retail team.
Apple – like Jigsaw, Ted Baker and
Karen Millen – is an 'aspirational'
brand that is almost as vital for
a development's success as the
anchor stores.

opposite
Liverpool ranked third in the national
league table of retail centres in the
early 1970s. By the late 1990s
the city had slipped to 17th. City
officials and Grosvenor hope that
the new development will put
Liverpool back among the UK's
premier shopping destinations.

Anchor stores are required to provide quality assurance, big brands and the range of products that will attract people to the development – without them, no development will be viable

The psychology of shopping – the John Lewis view

Margaret Jacques, the managing director of Liverpool's new John Lewis store, is used to upheaval. Jacques was the manager of the Manchester branch of Marks & Spencer which received the full force of the IRA bomb in 1996 and, having joined John Lewis in 2005, it was she who steered the move from Church Street to Hanover Place. Apart from simply reversing the decline of the old store, Jacques's role was to capitalise on both the new building and the wealth of the people who, it was hoped, would be tempted to shop in Liverpool's centre once again.

Part of the strategy, having got the store that customers wanted, was to organise products to best advantage. This involved a serious departure from standard practice. Menswear, for example, is located on ground level and is virtually the first thing customers see. 'Men are psychologically different from women when shopping. They don't want to walk very far,' says Jacques. But having taken the decision to make menswear so obvious, that begged a question – why not, then, locate computers and hi-fi equipment on the ground floor also? And if you do that, perhaps kitchen appliances should be there too? In fact, why not sell entire kitchens there? The result is a ground floor that is quantifiably different from that of any other large retailer, marked out by products that are typically located in basements or elsewhere which requires a special effort to reach them. 'It's been a riot,' said Jacques, three weeks after the store opened. 'All the indications are that everything we've done is being given a massive tick. The sale of fitted kitchens has rocketed.'

The location of other departments has also been given careful consideration. Homeware has been positioned next to the footbridge to the car park, allowing customers to haul heavy goods like rolled up rugs straight to their car (although people can now drive up to the collection point at the rear); the lighting department has been positioned so that, at night, the facade of the store is animated when viewed from the park; the restaurant and espresso bar, similarly, have been placed to provide eaters with park and river views.

'This is a prototype on which the business is going to base its expansion. It's a bit of an experiment, but what we learned in just a few hours is that we have the ability to sell top range items. In fact, the two things I told head office were: give me the right stock, and I'll sell it; also, I want to front load the store with staff,' says Jacques. The search for new employees has shown that it's not just customers who want to be here; 660 people worked in the old store and Jacques required an extra 280. She received more than 15,000 applications.

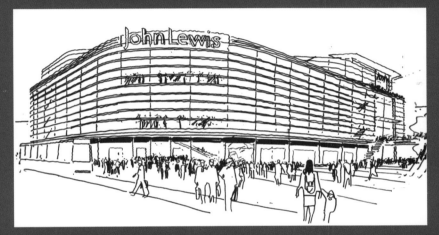

above

The residential tower in the centre of Liverpool One contains three major retailers on its lower levels: clothing stores Urban Outfitters and USC and Waterstone's, the bookshop. John Lewis can be glimpsed in the distance to the left.

The future of retail

'Shops must face up to growing competition for customers' cash from the internet and from experience-based activities such as holidays and sports,' wrote Richard Barkham, Grosvenor's group research director in *Retail Property Review*. 'Improved customer service and amenity along with complementary planning, transport and design policies are critical. All these factors must combine to make shopping places for people. Against this background, significant changes are already taking place in the way retail developments are planned, delivered and managed. The era of the cloned shopping mall will increasingly give way to a new generation of unique shopping places integrated into the urban townscape and featuring varied, locally relevant architecture and a more diverse mix of tenants.'

this page
This building, by Allies and Morrison architects, is successfully stratified into glazed retail units and stone-clad upper levels containing restaurants and the cinema entrance. This is the largest building in the development.

store which is the retail equivalent of BMW or Saab – brands including Karen Millen, Gieves & Hawkes, Zara, Apple. They are the sort of brands that, while available to most shoppers in price-tag terms, have a discernible whiff of high quality and classic modernity about them. Once the ink has dried on the contracts with the anchors, it is these brands that developers and letting agents turn to next.

The 1999 retail study that gave the city council the confidence to pursue a retail-led development of this scale concluded that Liverpool's main retail area could comfortably expand by around 1 million square feet (93,000 square metres). This figure was arrived at very carefully: any smaller and the development might not make the difference the city hoped for (smaller retail developments in the centre in recent decades had certainly failed to reverse Liverpool's decline), while a larger scheme

'Time and patience'

'Experience has taught us that the design of city-centre retail developments can be a long and complex process which will involve the balancing of a number of demands, many of which will seem to be in direct conflict with each other,' stated Grosvenor's expression of interest, submitted to Liverpool Council in August 1999. 'The resulting development will not be a single building, more a piece of the city centre comprising a selection of individual buildings. Time and patience will be needed to reach the correct solution. Once that solution has been achieved, its influence on a city such as Liverpool could be tremendously powerful. For many people the shopping district is the heart of the city. An attractive and innovative scheme for Bluecoat Triangle [the zone surrounding the Bluecoat Arts Centre] will revitalise Liverpool and act as a catalyst for further regeneration and the creation of wealth elsewhere in the city.'

could create an over-supply of shops and depress rental values. The new development had to be large, but not too large. As explained in chapter 2 (page 42), Grosvenor's masterplanning team, for very good design reasons including a commitment to the ideas of 'place-making', quickly set about injecting heavy doses of variety and vitality into the development zone. But these principles had to work in retail terms too. Running in parallel with the masterplanning efforts was a consultation exercise which eventually sought the views of 10,000 people (mainly potential consumers, who continue to be consulted) to determine space requirements and the right retail mix and adjacencies. Quite apart from the criteria which should come as standard in any new development like this (access, safety, cleanliness, location, service and product range), these phone calls, questionnaires and focus groups found that a sensitive approach to scale should lie at the heart of the project. 'People hate uniformity,' says Jenefer Greenwood. Thankfully, these findings supported the designers' view that this project should be more than a shopping mall without a roof, that the main streets should be genuinely distinctive. The size and form of the retail units themselves have also been influenced by this consultation programme. Apart from the anchor stores and major space users, Liverpool One provides a range of shop units from 300 square feet (28 square metres) to 5,000 square feet (465 square metres) on both single and multiple levels. This is a relatively unusual

below
The footbridge linking John Lewis with the Liver Street car park. During daylight hours, the bridge is bathed in a white light, in sympathy with the John Lewis brand; at night, when the store is closed, the bridge is illuminated in red.

By May 2008, 80 per cent of
the units were either occupied
or let; the entire development
was 92 per cent let by October

The multi-coloured kiosk within one of the development's arcades is an intensely post-modern addition to the new streetscape. Inspired by whimsical tiling and brickwork found elsewhere in the city, the kiosk adds an unexpected splash of colour to this new cut-through.

opposite
'Malls without walls'. Modern shopping centres need not be enclosed, although some of the organisational principles behind them might well be shared. In Liverpool, shoppers can never forget they are at the centre of a large, waterside metropolis. There is nothing artificial about Liverpool One.

(but increasingly popular) shop type because retailers have traditionally preferred to trade on just a single floor. Most importantly, though, this desire for variety played into the hands of the design team which was already planning to tackle the 42 acre site by dividing it into discrete zones, outlined earlier. In retail terms, the five zones came to be characterised thus:

- Paradise Street: 'urban fashion', featuring brands such as Nike, Cult and Urban Outfitters;
- Hanover Street: 'suburban comfort', with homeware stores and a mix of uses including offices and a budget hotel;
- Peter's Lane: high quality fashion and boutiques such as Ted Baker and Jigsaw;
- South John Street: family-centred, mid-market shopping comprising fashion brands with broad appeal as well as music and other 'High Street' dependables such as Esprit, Gap, Superdrug and WH Smith;
- The Park: the prime leisure element, including bars, restaurants and a 14 screen Odeon cinema.

The importance of getting the retail mix right and attracting the interest of tenants cannot be overstated, not least because the funding deal with Grosvenor's development partners was conditional upon securing leases for the two anchor stores, the three car parks and the cinema. Once done, agents could then set about securing leases on the remainder of the scheme. Committing John Lewis and Debenhams to the anchor stores was a relatively straightforward (if lengthy) process, while there was no shortage of car park operators queueing up to take on the three multi-storeys that were planned, and Netherlands-based Q-Park was selected by Grosvenor for the quality of its service. Securing a cinema tenant proved trickier, however, and long and complicated discussions with a large operator broke down over a range of issues including design details and commercial terms. Fortunately, the

'The era of the cloned shopping mall
will increasingly give way to a new
generation of unique shopping places
integrated into the urban townscape
and featuring varied, locally relevant
architecture and a more diverse mix
of tenants,' says Grosvenor's group
research director, Richard Barkham.

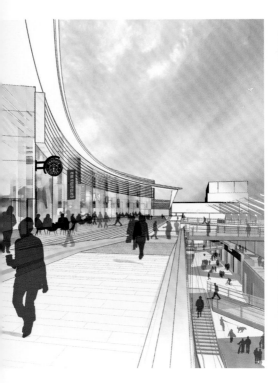

Odeon had shown continual interest and stepped in to take the re-designed 14-screen cinema, allowing Grosvenor to proceed with a funded scheme.

With tenants found for the principal components of the masterplan, that left 175 retail and leisure units to fill. Many retailers virtually came knocking on the door: 'They'd be mad not to,' said David Quinn, northern editor of property journal the *Estates Gazette*. However, not everyone was so easily convinced. Some retailers were already a little too entrenched elsewhere in the region and were reluctant to open new stores that might compete with existing branches; others, from outside the area, were sceptical about the idea of investing in the city. 'Some people just do not get Liverpool,' says Greenwood, who remembers taking one London-based retailer to view the site. 'He was completely surprised. "You need to get more people up here," he told me. "This is just awesome."' There were even retailers who turned their noses up at what they believed (in spite of all the evidence to the contrary) was to be a shopping mall. What makes the job of the leasing team particularly tricky is the herd mentality of many retailers; a store will take up space in a development if rival, or complementary, operations have already made a commitment. Expressions of interest can be easy to come by, but translating them into contracts can be difficult and excruciating. And then there is the matter of adjacencies – who is next to whom. Some retailers can be very picky about who their neighbours are, and they may even press particularly hard to secure one plot rather than another. It is a very difficult puzzle to solve, not least because the big brands (the luxury names and those 'aspirational' stores) know only too well that a development needs them as much as they need it. Preferential treatment, or one-off deals, for particular stores is a fact of life. What is remarkable is that more than half of the names brought into the project are new to the city, including Apple and fashion retailers Bank, Cult, Nike, American Apparel, German chain Esprit and Spanish store Pull & Bear. 'To achieve the right solution we believe that the city

More than half of the names brought into the project are new to Liverpool, including Apple and fashion retailers Bank, Cult, Nike, American Apparel and German chain Esprit

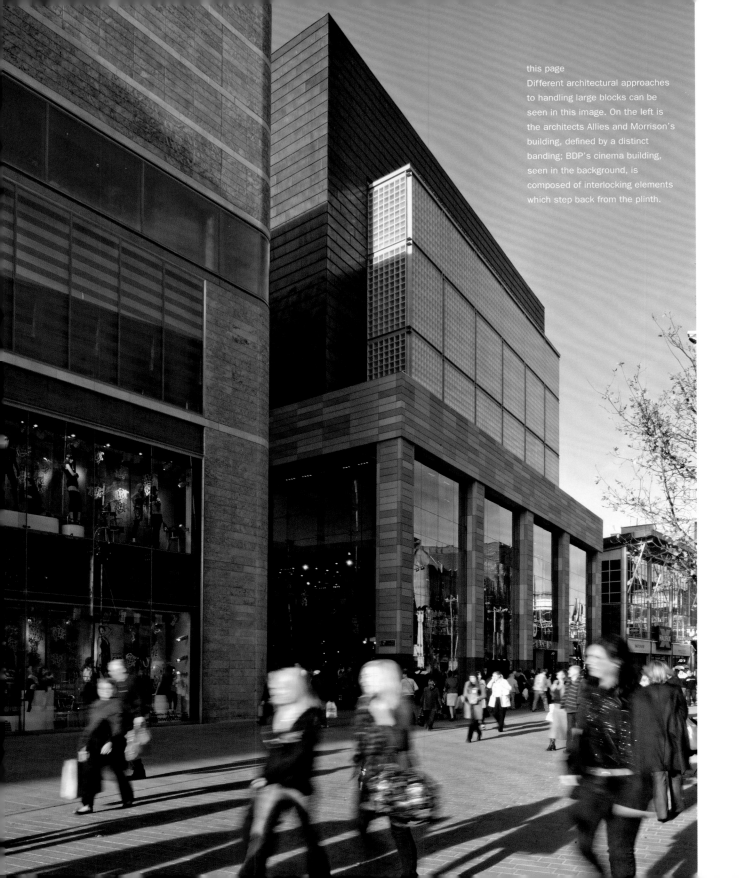

this page
Different architectural approaches
to handling large blocks can be
seen in this image. On the left is
the architects Allies and Morrison's
building, defined by a distinct
banding; BDP's cinema building,
seen in the background, is
composed of interlocking elements
which step back from the plinth.

this page
Peter's Lane arcade by architects
Dixon Jones. Michael Burchnall, a
senior planning official at Liverpool
City Council, calls this project 'one
of the most dramatic buildings'
within the wider development.

needs to secure major new stores not currently represented in Liverpool,' said Grosvenor's original expression of interest to the city council, dated August 1999. 'An approach that focused on merely re-ordering the existing offer would be wrong.' By the time Phase One was opened on 29 May 2008, 80 per cent of the units were either occupied or let; the entire development was 92 per cent let by the following October.

Crucially, in spite of the economic downturn that was looming as the development neared completion, rental values were coming in broadly on target. Retailers and letting agents use the phrase 'in terms of zone A' (ITZA) when describing rental values, which measures the price per square foot to a depth of 20 feet (6 metres) into the store. This 'zone A' slice of any shop floor is the most attractive and therefore most expensive part of the property, and it is this premier value that developers want to maximise. In Church Street, Liverpool's traditional prime shopping pitch, 'zone A' rates tend to be a shade over £320 per square foot (0.09 sqaure metres); before it even opened, the lower level of South John Street had reached £315 per square foot (ITZA), while the upper level was nearer £290. The new stores around the corner on the brand new Paradise Street were being let at much the same figure.

Securing John Lewis

John Lewis is the anchor store of choice, and any retail-led development will be on a reasonably secure footing if this venerable British brand can be persuaded to participate. The thing is, John Lewis knows this. 'We achieve higher sales densities – pounds per square foot – than any other store operator,' says Gareth Thomas, the company's director of retail and development. 'Without being arrogant, we attract people like no other retailer can, so with us Grosvenor can be confident that their development will attract people from far and wide. If a developer can get us into their scheme, they can charge a premium to other retailers.' The company also has another card to play – its longevity. John Lewis, which is a partnership and therefore insulated from the instability of share prices, considers itself less vulnerable to the shock of recession. It can therefore offer a developer something more than just footfall. 'Other retailers are motivated by more short-term pressures by

above

Indicative sketch of the lower end of Paradise Street, with John Lewis mapped out with a series of pencil strokes. The tenants are fictional, but the form of the building is exactly as delivered.

left
A further study of Paradise Street.
In spite of the size of this large block,
it is broken into discrete elements in
an effort to minimise uniformity.

The new development needed
to encourage affluent consumers
from Liverpool's suburbs and
outer fringes to shop in the
city centre

being listed on the stock market. We can afford to take a longer view and talk to developers about projects which won't mature for another eight, 10 or 12 years. We can be sure we'll be around then. And that's attractive to developers,' says Gareth Thomas.

By the same token, John Lewis needed to move – desperately. The company had been located in Liverpool for many decades, occupying the former George Henry Lee store on Church Street. Although prime pitch territory, George Henry Lee was an amalgam of elderly premises with a veneer of respectability that obscured serious shortcomings in trading terms. There were over 40 different floor levels, catering facilities were insufficient, daylight didn't penetrate very far and the customer pick-up desk was not accessible by car. This last point is actually a major issue for John Lewis. In spite of a multi-million pound make-over and rebrand, as well as the introduction of seven-days-a-week opening, the store was among the least profitable of the partnership's branches, and it was never far away from being a loss-maker. So the decision to up sticks and move into a new custom-designed building down the road was 'a pretty straightforward one' says Gareth Thomas. Trouble was, the company needed to be convinced that Grosvenor could actually pull off the development because the land assembly and almost certain use of compulsory purchase orders would mean entering a legal minefield: 'We were interested in this scheme right at the beginning, but my reservation was to do with the complexity of it all. I was doubtful that the developer would be able to acquire enough land to be able to make the scheme viable,' says Thomas. 'It's not uncommon for a developer in the UK to talk about significant regeneration as

below
Officials at the city council were initially sceptical about the idea of an arcade, which they worried might appear too mall-like or exclusive. But the architects considered this form of building to be a useful one for the site – the scale of buildings at either end of this little street are entirely different, and an arcade mediates between the two neatly.

below right
These shopfronts, in bronze, deliberately reference an earlier age of shopping. Behind the stores, though, is an underground access route for deliveries and other services.

this page
Peter's Lane arcade, striking for its
curving roof washed with daylight, is
tenanted largely by upper end retail
brands: Fat Face, Ted Baker and
Jones Bootmaker, for example.

opposite

Seen from Manesty's Lane, the
glazing of John Lewis contrasts
with the more solid materials of
neighbouring buildings. Its curving
front responds to the path of a
tram line, which was planned for the
site but cancelled by the city council.

a consequence of their investment. But the best example I can think of where this has proven to be the case is what Grosvenor has achieved in Liverpool. We just had to buy into Grosvenor's vision.' The board decision to make the move was taken in October 2003. The commercial terms that sealed the deal are confidential, but it is certain that John Lewis got itself a reasonable settlement, including a commitment from Grosvenor to buy their old store. John Lewis is a shrewd and tough negotiator. The company even managed to emblazon its name across a multistorey car park which is neither owned nor operated by them; the spatial standards to which the car park was designed are also John Lewis's.

For John Lewis, this is literally their dream store. For some years the company had been doing a lot of work on store design, involving customer consultation exercises and visits to the world's premier retailers. From out of this research emerged a blueprint for a new kind of store – one that traded over no more than four floors, maximised the use of natural light, had no basement (customers don't like them), provided a variety of access points, offered toilet facilities on every floor, and (of course) was located close to car parks and transport nodes. The new store at Liverpool One has the lot. 'I have no reservations about this shop. It's terrific,' says Thomas. 'This is the first shop where we've been able to apply the theory of our perfect store absolutely purely.'

The John Lewis store is the only building in this large development which is self-contained – it has no party walls and stands in its own space (other than the footbridge and a basement which is part of the sub-ground megastructure). The quality of the urban realm is therefore especially important for the success of this building, and it is interesting to hear Gareth Thomas talk about the links between a successful masterplan and profitable retailing. Although the company does operate a handful of stores in shopping malls, the majority of its branches are part of a street scene, and all the company's new stores on the drawing board are located in city centres. 'We don't operate in a vacuum. What matters is what shoppers think,' he says. 'The colour, vibrancy, vitality and variety of Liverpool One is a positive. It's something shoppers will enjoy. I think they're going to have a sufficiently good experience here that they'll want to return. Grosvenor's challenge is to keep the quality of its development sufficiently high.'

Privatised space

In a self-contained shopping mall, this is a relatively easy thing to do, but city centres ('malls without walls') are more tricky to manage – especially in terms of maintaining cleanliness, safety and an overall coherence. Part of the solution in Liverpool was for the city council to part privatise the Paradise Street Development Area by allowing Grosvenor to manage the site through a series of 'public realm arrangements'. In practice, the settlement is relatively benign, but it has proved to be a controversial measure in some circles, largely over the matter of principle that a commercial enterprise be granted the controls ordinarily lodged with a public authority. In 2006 the Royal Institution of Chartered Surveyors stirred things up with a report titled *What Kind of World Are We Building? The Privatisation of Public Space* in which author Anna Minton argued that developers were sterilising inner-city spaces by replicating the values of shopping malls. 'The Grosvenor example has aroused particular controversy because it appears to be the first time that an entire city centre is to be privatised,' Minton wrote.

The media, of course, picked up on the report and ran alarmist articles predicting gated developments policed by privatised forces of 'sheriffs'. The *Sunday Times*, quoting the report almost verbatim, suggested that 'vagrants, skateboarders, unruly gangs of youths and demonstrators can all expect to be turned away at its entrances'. Remarks like these have become a source of pain and frustration to those closely involved with the project, largely because critics tend to forget that the

The brand

For most of the life of this development, it was referred to as the 'Paradise Project'. During 2005 branding consultants began work on a name that would have a resonance outside of Liverpool. The intention was to add to the allure of the scheme by marking it out as a destination of some distinction. Part of the discussion, interestingly, was whether it needed a name at all. If integration and permeability were such strong features of BDP's masterplan, shouldn't the same principles apply to the way the project was perceived? Why call it anything? The Paradise Project was, after all, simply a new district of Liverpool.

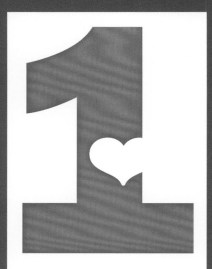

LIABILITY
**LIVERPOOL
ONE**
Love the City

Ayo Daramola-Martin, Grosvenor's marketing director, who led the branding and promotion of the project, expects that the development will eventually be subsumed within the wider brand that is 'Liverpool'. But retailers needed to be persuaded that 'this was no ordinary shopping centre' and that it was being conceived, designed, built and maintained as a distinct entity. What was needed was something meaningful, memorable and concise. After engaging branding firm Wolff Olins, a shortlist of three names was drawn up and 'Liverpool One' emerged as the final candidate. The name also went hand-in-hand with a set of six new 'rules' drawn up to describe the freshness and zest Grosvenor was aiming to bring to the new city centre: make new rules; involve everyone; love the city; think big; create more; and be the best.

The name was just the start. Next came the logo and a multi-media public relations and marketing campaign which went on to win a property industry award. 'Liverpool One was streets ahead of the pack in the retail category, with a hard-working, unified and coherent marketing strategy', reported the *Estates Gazette* in April 2007. 'Liverpool One keeps its clever brand values strong and memorable across all the different routes to market that it employs and the end result is professionalism itself. Once seen, never forgotten.'

In the meantime, digital modellers GMJ had been busy creating a fully three-dimensional, virtual version of the emerging development. This project alone took two years, but it allowed retailers to take a step forward in time, to inspect the site in extraordinary detail and get a feel for what it would look like post-completion; they could look up, down, around, zoom in and out, and even see their proposed store against the context of the wider scheme in photo-realistic resolution. The idea of 'place' was being established long before Liverpool One actually existed. A certain attitude was slowly being created.

development is about using private money to rebuild the city centre – and the scheme is anything but gated. The streets are as new as the buildings and Grosvenor is keen to protect its investment. Argent, the property firm developing King's Cross in London, is thinking along much the same lines. Furthermore, the city council always planned for a degree of privatisation; the city retains the freehold on the site but granted Grosvenor a 250-year lease, during which time the company is expected to match the quality of the estate with the standard of its management. At Liverpool One, Grosvenor has committed to maintaining, lighting, cleaning and managing the entire development largely because the city council could not commit to reaching the level of service the investors insist upon; indeed, this was part of the attraction to many of the retailers who have taken up space there. The city also benefits from levying a substantial ground rent on Grosvenor (5 per cent of the rent paid by tenants) which contributes to its annual income by many millions. Michael Burchnall from the city council defended the strategy on BBC Radio 4 and in *Planning* magazine.

The reality bears him out. There is little or no evidence the public has experienced the effect of the ownership/management strategy other than to notice that a great deal of care is being taken of Liverpool One. 'What people are looking for is a fabulous environment, which includes ease of access, security and cleanliness,' says Grosvenor's Jenefer Greenwood. 'I think this development is exceptional, which is probably an over-used word. Another overused word is "unique", but this is a retail development with a five-acre, city centre park. It really is unique. So we need to look after it very carefully.'

Chapter 5
ARCHITECTURE

Chapter 5
ARCHITECTURE

The pool of architects

Liverpool One was always going to deliver variety. Quite apart from other fundamental principles, such as naturally extending the city's existing retail area and respecting original street patterns, Grosvenor intended to explore the idea of 'buildings in the city'. It was the notion that a variation in scale, composition, materiality and architectural 'language' could add up to an urban experience that felt humane – a city centre that could be by turns grand and intimate, bustling and rather relaxed. The new buildings would be part of the fabric of the place, and the very idea of being *in* Liverpool (rather than merely within a development which happened to be located there) underwrote everything. This project was to have, like any successful urban centre, a completeness about it that resisted uniformity. There was to be nothing monolithic about Liverpool One; and the faceless shopping mall was a non-starter.

'As a property developer, I'd spent too much time apologising for the 1960s,' says John Bullough, former retail director of Grosvenor who was instrumental in getting the developer appointed. 'I wanted to get people together who were fired up by this idea of creating real places, not mega-malls.'

Neither was pastiche or artificial diversity an option. Commissioning a single architect to produce a variable design would have been easy, but clumsy. At the outset Grosvenor knew that genuine diversity could be achieved only through the efforts of more than one designer – perhaps as many

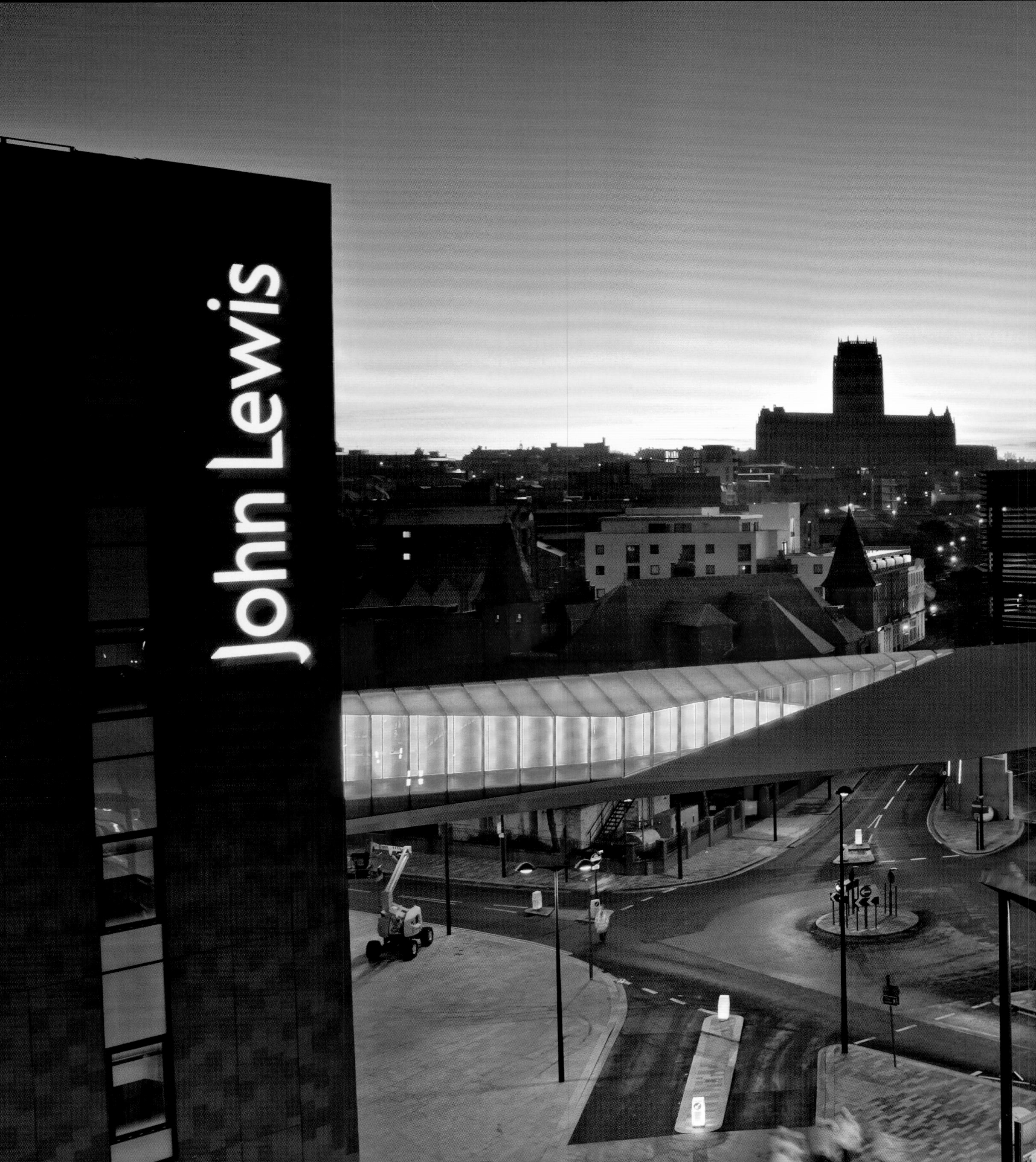
John Lewis

Liverpool One Remaking a city centre

The masterplan creates several new places, not one large development; that responds to the needs and aspirations of all kinds of people

as half a dozen. That way, the distinctive approaches of different firms would be brought to bear on the masterplan; the styles, values and thought processes would vary, but the parameters outlined by BDP would lend it all a certain coherence. When Rod Holmes joined the team he thoroughly embraced the idea of using a multiplicity of architects. In fact, he used 26 of them.

The masterplan, said the brief issued to architects throughout 2004, was one that 'creates several new places, not one large development; that provides the scope for a new architecture that is varied, but always of the highest quality; and that responds to the needs and aspirations of all kinds of people. In order to achieve this "buildings in the city" approach, the most appropriate and talented designers of local, regional, national and international standing are being selected to create buildings of individual character and quality'. It was an approach that attracted the instant support of English Heritage, the government-funded body which has a statutory right to be consulted on developments in historically sensitive or significant areas. 'This is the single-most important point within the masterplan. The use of different architectural practices captures some of the historic

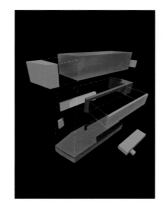

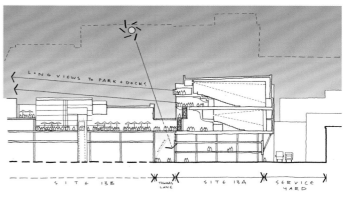

right
Early sketch, by Aedas, mapping
out the form of the Hilton hotel.
Even at this early stage, the building
conforms to the gentle curve set out
in the masterplan.

The use of 26 architecture practices has created a development that is very definitely Liverpudlian rather than 'anywhereville'

character, distinctiveness and diversity that developed throughout the area over time. From that point of view full marks to Grosvenor,' says Henry Owen-John, regional director for the North-West at English Heritage. The result, he says, is a development that is very definitely Liverpudlian rather than 'anywhereville'.

The full list of participating practices is an interesting one. It's not exactly a 'who's who' but it is a pretty accurate cross-section of the architectural profession, including large, well-established firms; small, up-and-coming ones; international names; and niche studios whose reputations go well

below

Plot by Plot. Liverpool One was divided into discrete plots, each handled by a different architect:
1 Dixon Jones
2 Page\Park
3a, 3b Haworth Tompkins
4a, 4b2, 4c Brock Carmichael
4b1 Owen Ellis Partnership

5a, 5b Stephenson Bell
5aa (facade) Hawkins\Brown
6 Glenn Howells Architects
7, 7a Haworth Tompkins
8 Greig and Stephenson (with kiosk unit by FAT)
9 CZWG
10 John McAslan + Partners

10a Wilkinson Eyre
11 Aedas and Squire & Partners
12 Pelli Clarke Pelli Architects, with Brock Carmichael
13b Allies and Morrison
13c, 13d Building Design Partnership
14 Building Design Partnership (facade by Marks Barfield)

15 Groupe 6
16f Building Design Partnership
16g Studio Three
17, 17a Wilkinson Eyre
18 To be determined
19, 20 Austin-Smith:Lord
21, 22 To be determined
Water feature Gross Max

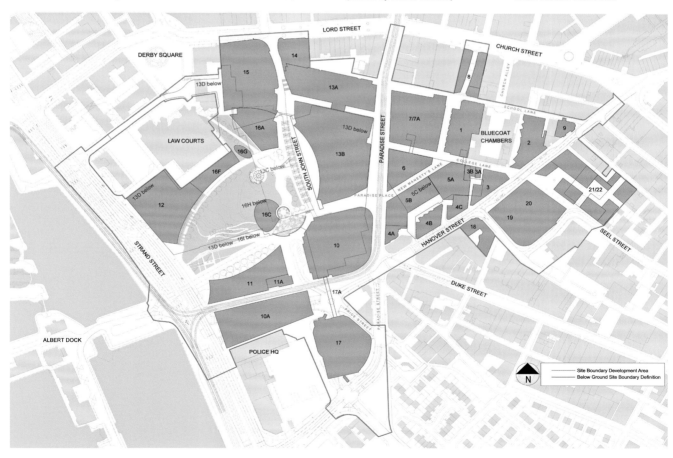

this page
John Lewis, by John McAslan +
Partners. This store was carefully
planned as distinct zones: a set of
glassy trading floors, and a more
solid, rectilinear block at the rear
accommodating services, offices
and storage.

John Lewis

John Lewis

John Lewis

The Compass

beyond their size. Some are barely known outside the north-west of England. One or two practices were even replaced. Rod Holmes actually made it his business to avoid architects with particular expertise, especially in the retail sector. He wanted to challenge his architects and make them think, rather than allow them to produce work effortlessly. Dixon Jones, better known for cultural work like the Royal Opera House, was commissioned for a small row of shops; Allies and Morrison, best known for office work and its reinvention of the Royal Festival Hall, was appointed to design the largest retail and leisure block in the whole development; two times Stirling Prize-winning practice Wilkinson Eyre, designer of the Gateshead Millennium Bridge which quickly became an icon for the North-East, was commissioned to design a multistorey car park. (So successful has that particular design been that the practice is now having to turn down car park work.)

It would appear that nobody within Grosvenor wanted a simple life. In a couple of cases, architects were commissioned to design just facades – leaving the actual buildings behind them to be designed by someone else (a highly unconventional and tricky relationship to manage). Amassing the architects to bring this project to life was an exercise in horses for courses: some were hand picked; others had to pitch for the work through invited competitions; a pavilion in the park was always going to be the work of a small Liverpool practice. Moreover, not all design firms were subjected to the executive architect regime. By and large, architects would take their designs up to concept stage and hand them over to BDP for detailing; but architects working on particularly sensitive sites, especially those who worked up detailed schemes very early in the project, were permitted to see their projects right through to completion. For example, Page\Park (the BBC building) and CZWG (the 'Bling Bling' building) did their own detailing. Most, including Allies and Morrison (the central block between Paradise and South John Streets) and John McAslan + Partners (John Lewis), didn't. Some relationships between concept and executive architect worked better than others, and in retrospect Grosvenor should have formalised these relations rather than left them to individual architects.

this page
Sandstone, glass block and
stainless steel. BDP set lighter
materials atop a heavy plinth to
make this large building melt into
the sky. The smattering of polished
steel panels was inspired by the
sparkle of the sun on water.

The briefs issued to architects were incredibly specific, including not only the precise sizes and volumes of buildings but also the ways that reports and drawings should be presented. Every architect needs to respond to constraints in order to test their creativity, but the parameters needn't be so restrictive that there's little for them to do. So masterplanners BDP, who wrote these briefing documents, had to describe in excruciating detail exactly what was required (and, indeed, permitted) without tying the hands of the concept architects too much. To make matters trickier, very few sites in Liverpool One contain isolated, self-contained buildings – most touch their neighbours – and architects were expected to work in a spirit of collaboration, mindful of what their colleagues were up to next door without feeling the need to imitate it or become too upset when they didn't like what they saw. 'Unless you had control and influence on the overall plan, you had to quickly focus on your own project. You had to make the jump from the larger scale to working much more locally, and not get too excited about what was happening to other elements in the project,' says Sir Jeremy Dixon of Dixon Jones architects.

Scope for creativity

Dixon's project is something of a microcosm for Liverpool One generally. It links contrasting zones within the development; it strives for both contextualism and innovation; and it benefits from a particular attention to detail. The original brief called for two-storey shops to line both sides of Peter's Lane, a route that skirts the edge of the Grade 1 listed Bluecoat Arts Centre to link School Lane, with its warehouse-scale buildings, and College Lane, characterised by far smaller frontages. Sir Jeremy Dixon's instinct was to create a covered arcade, a neat device which negotiated the shift in scale by simply ignoring it. The arcade (a tunnel by another name) becomes a transitional space, allowing visitors a certain surprise and delight in what they find at either end. The trouble was, the city council wasn't keen.

Dixon has long been interested in the development of cities, and what fascinates him in particular are the 'typologies' of urban design – the squares, crescents, terraces, blocks and streets that provide the jigsaw pieces from which towns and cities are assembled. The arcade, he says, is one of these typologies, a long-established form of covered street which has fallen out of fashion in recent years. 'We have always been interested in arcades. One of the attractions of the arcade is that it is a special condition of "the street" in which the designer has greater overall control. It was with particular pleasure that we had the opportunity of looking again at this fascinating building

below
Elevation of College Lane, by Haworth Tompkins Architects. Elderly warehouse buildings are preserved and flanked by contemporary structures which are both sympathetic and confident within this historic context.

below right
Elevation detail of Haworth Tompkins' retail/residential building on Paradise Street. The practice first came to the attention of Rod Holmes as winner of the UK's 'Young Architect of the Year' award in 2001.

The briefs issued to architects were incredibly specific, including not only the precise sizes and volumes of buildings but also the ways that reports and drawings should be presented

above
The defining feature of the Peter's
Lane arcade is the curved roof,
illuminated by sunshine. The
roof glows even under cloud
cover. Polished granite reflects
adjacent buildings.

type,' says Dixon. The problem, though, was that the arcade was ever so slightly suggestive of the shopping mall – the sort of controlled, internalised space that was anathema to the entire project. Rod Holmes understood the idea almost instantly, so Dixon's challenge was to convince local officials. His tactic was simple: to make the arcade beautiful. He widened it a little, to emphasise the fact that it still belonged to the 'public realm'; he proposed to use bronze in the detailing of the shop fronts; he placed little public squares at either end; and, probably most importantly, he capped the arcade with a curved roof awash with daylight. Dixon has also used other touches to reinforce a sense of place: at one end polished granite reflects the historic textures of neighbouring buildings; at the other end the roof line drops down to frame the cupola atop the Bluecoat building.

Dixon got his arcade and its resolution shows that city officials had nothing to worry about. Indeed, this little street would hardly be the same without its quarter-curve of a roof and the play of daylight admitted through the single clerestory window. The effect of daylight on a white surface, even when overcast, is remarkable – an effect tested by Dixon who stuck his head into a scale model of the arcade, mounted on a wheelbarrow, on London's Primrose Hill. 'A model provides a surprisingly similar effect to the real building,' says Dixon. 'There isn't a scale with light. Light performs identically whether in a model or in a building.'

this page
Demonstration sketch of the way
this arcade handles light. Daylight
is reflected off a white surface on an
adjacent building, and enters through
a clerestory window.

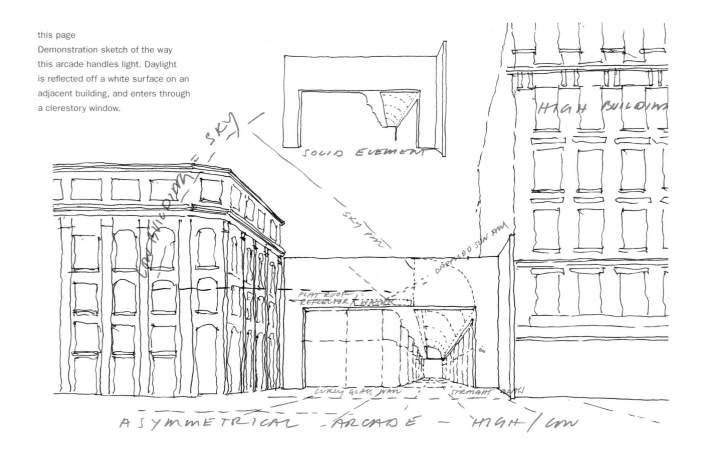

Peter's Lane would hardly be the same without its quarter-curve of a roof and the play of daylight admitted through the single clerestory window

this page
The College Lane elevation of
Dixon Jones' arcade is deliberately
modulated to frame the cupola of the
nearby Bluecoat Arts Centre. Views
and glimpses of historic Liverpool are
littered throughout this development.

below
The canopy over the restaurant
zone of South John Street. This
element was designed almost as a
dock-like structure, a piece of heavy,
utilitarian metalwork.

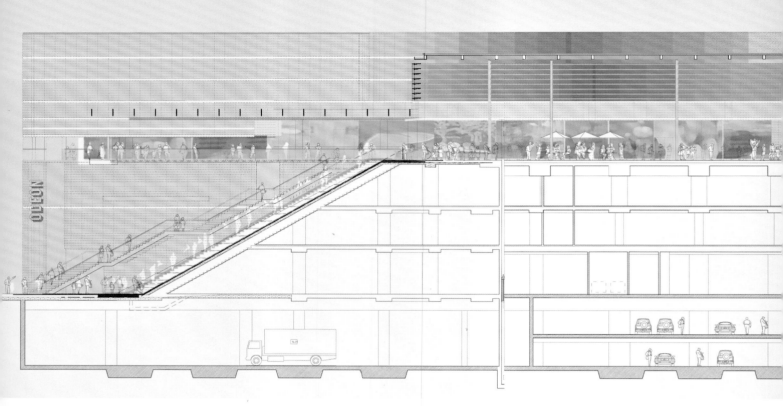

above
Sectional drawing from Paradise
Street (on the left) through to South
John Street and the park (right).
Invisible to most visitors to Liverpool
One is the vast underground car park
and service facility.

The architects of the largest single component of Liverpool One, the retail and leisure block that straddles Paradise and South John Streets, also managed to carve out a similar degree of creativity from what would appear to be a brief with little room for manoeuvre. Allies and Morrison took on a project that actually looked worse than restrictive. Quite apart from the size and massing that had been established in the masterplan, this plot sits above the new underground car park and service road, so ventilation shafts and lifts run right through the building at predetermined and non-negotiable points. And to add insult to injury, the masterplan also provided for the building to be carved away at two key points – one to open up views to the Anglican Cathedral, and another (far deeper) cut to provide glimpses of the Liver Building. Furthermore, construction of the building's foundations had begun before the designs had been completed, removing any flexibility for structural change. 'We loved the challenge,' remembers Tim Makower, partner at Allies and Morrison, who considers the project to be more of an urban block than a building. 'The big question for us was in finding harmony, finding beauty. We did have to wonder at times.'

Makower's starting point was the topography of Liverpool, and the strata that had been laid down to provide the rocky foundations of the city, including the promontory on which the castle once stood overlooking the docks. This building was to be a large one, and breaking its functions and composition into distinct, 'stratified' bands would help to break it up and reduce its bulk. The stone metaphor was also useful because this building (or urban block) sits right at the centre of

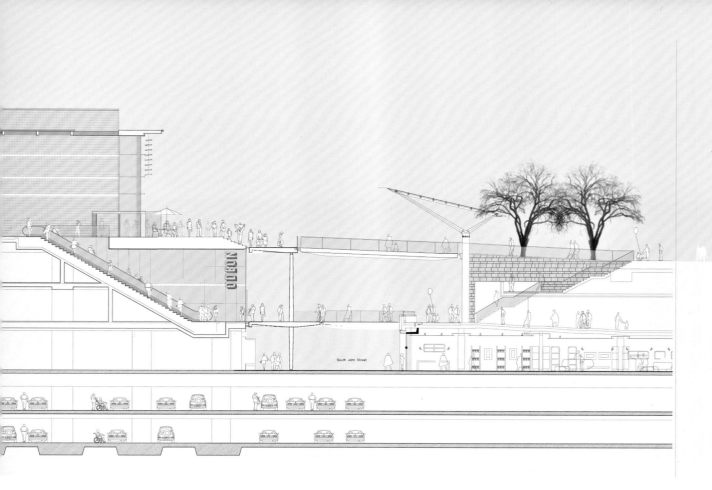

A search for solidity runs
deep throughout Liverpool One.
The use of stone is widespread.
Even the massive glass facade
of Debenhams is glacially opaque

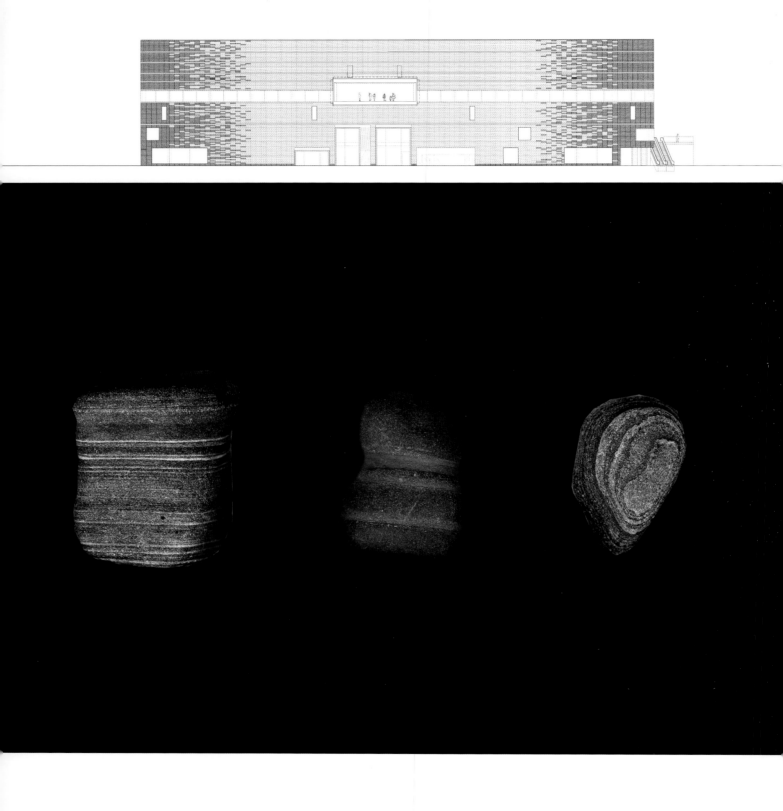

left
Wall Street elevation of the Allies and Morrison building, which occupies plot 13b. The building is virtually cut in two by a horizontal band which separates the retail functions of the ground floors from the leisure spaces above. The cinema bridge can be seen in the centre of the drawing.

left
Strata. Allies and Morrison took inspiration from these north Wales pebbles, which demonstrate how a single, monolithic unit can be beautifully broken up into discrete elements. These stones helped the architects find a solution for site 13b, the largest building in Liverpool One.

The Liverpool swagger
Paul Finch, architecture critic

The architecture of Liverpool One derives from a refreshing and radical change in thinking about urban shopping. Instead of a US-style mall, imposed as though it were an alien invader, Grosvenor took the enlightened decision to create a retail experience based largely on the street patterns and grain of the existing city. The result is a series of street blocks, most designed by a different architectural hand, that gives huge character to a substantial new quarter. You can find shelter in arcades or under canopies, but the shopping experience is all about walking, fresh air and views both of the immediate architecture and of the wider city. Split levels are deployed intelligently, while the creation of Chavasse Park and the route it embraces links extremely well with the Albert Dock, which had always seemed rather cut off from the city centre.

Grosvenor's Rod Holmes had the unenviable task of managing 26 different architectural practices of varying attitude and approach; on the evidence of the excellent trading now boosting the city centre's fortunes, the result has proved well worth it. If one had a reservation about the approach adopted, it was that the result might be something of an architectural zoo. Happily, clarity of circulation and some very good landscaping (soft and hard), have created a background in which good quality individual buildings can co-exist without competing as meaningless icons.

The proximity of the docks, and indeed the Mersey, required that this development have a certain scale, a certain grandeur, a certain Liverpudlian swagger: 'We are as good as anybody'. Cesar Pelli's residential block on the edge of the site provides just that; further into the development the splendid stone used on the Allies and Morrison building is a reminder of the extraordinary architectural tradition of Liverpool in the 19th and early 20th centuries. Even the car park, bridge link and bus station, by Wilkinson Eyre, are confident designs rather than municipal apologies.

Liverpool now seems to have a new swagger of its own. This is partly because of its European Capital of Culture status in 2008 and partly because of the successful Art Biennial, but not least it is because its new shopping heart at last provides the city centre with the variety of contemporary architectural quality it has long lacked.

the development and it was always the intention of architect, masterplanner and developer that it appear as something lasting, substantial – a sort of anchor. Makower refers to it as 'a reformatted piece of geology'. The design team eventually settled on Scheinsberg limestone from Germany for the facade; this is a stone which looks, says Makower, like 'ugly canned meat' when polished but takes on a heavy, granite-like appearance when hammered, as it is here. Portland stone has been used for the bands which run horizontally around the upper portion of the building, above a heavily shadowed third-storey slot which the architects refer to as the plateau. In spite of the two-storey glazing, there is something of north Wales' Carnarvon Castle about this project.

A search for solidity runs deep throughout Liverpool One. The use of limestone, granite, brick, concrete and terracotta is widespread, and even the massive glass facade of Debenhams is glacially opaque. The contrasting glassiness of John Lewis is still stratified by a marked banding, much like

Liverpool One Remaking a city centre

the Allies and Morrison building, and its strident curves suggest rock formations sculpted by the wind. Notwithstanding the razor sharpness of Glenn Howells' building which fills the triangular plot between Paradise Street and New Manesty's Lane, much of the development is contoured in this way. There is a roundedness to the western part of the development, with echoes of the dockside from which any sharp lines have long been eroded, that speaks of weathering and the forces of nature. The immensity of the steps which sweep up into the park, as thoroughly artificial as anything else on the site, communicates a certain longevity; it is as if these steps are meant to be there, that they have always been there, and that they could not have been resolved in any other way. It is an architecture of toughness, like much that is found in this city. The Anglican Cathedral, St George's Hall, the Three Graces, the Albert Dock, the Georges Dock ventilation building, the warehouses ... all are expressions of robustness, among many other things. And even the deep, dark railway cutting into Lime Street Station is referenced by the Piranesian chasm and criss-crossing bridges of South John Street ('It's not Piranesian enough!' says Allies and Morrison's Tim Makower). None of this is the architecture of the crazy shape or experimental material. It is a sober and very grounded demonstration of 21st-century design, an approach that puts a premium on place-making instead of the architectural icon.

But then, this being Liverpool, Grosvenor has allowed itself to relax and inject the occasional dose of quirkiness into all this masonry and muscle. Colourful, whimsical flourishes pop up all over the place, from Marks Barfield's screen of multi-coloured tubes which wrap around the surface of a Costa Coffee shop, to the Postmodern mischief of the retail pavilion by FAT (Fashion Architecture Taste). The pedestrian bridge linking John Lewis to the adjacent car park could so easily have been, well, pedestrian; but Wilkinson Eyre has produced a play of faceted surfaces that is both delightful and structurally intriguing. It is this approach which underpinned Grosvenor's appointment strategy – architects were expected to add value to the brief by bringing something clever and wholly unexpected to it, where appropriate.

Just compare the neutral language of the brief to architects CZWG with the building that was actually delivered: 'There is the possibility of an imaginative treatment to the corner,' stated the brief, dated 23 March 2004. 'The elevational treatment of the building must respond to the high profile of the site. Its strong corner location ... requires a confident design of appropriate status within the street.' CZWG's answer was the 'Bling Bling' building, an exuberant and glittering

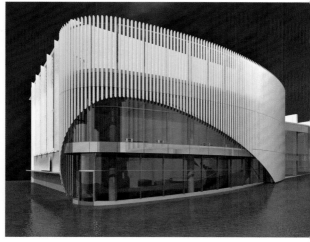

PSDA – SITE 9 (SCHEME 1)

ensemble which takes the humble bay window and pumps it up to arresting proportions. The tenant was a force to be reckoned with. Herbert Howe is Liverpool's most high-profile hairdresser – he drives a white Cadillac and wears pink at public functions when everyone else is in grey – and his Paradise Street salon was earmarked for demolition in Grosvenor's masterplan. Rod Holmes decided to find an architect who would be a match for Howe's verve, irreverence and that hint of excess. Hence the call to Piers Gough. When architect and tenant met, Howe asked about the boxy projections that appeared in the drawings. 'We call them our blings,' replied Gough, a term which was seized upon by Howe, giving the building a name and ensuring that it got built incredibly close to the original vision. But for all its chutzpah, and the fact that 'Bling' is repeatedly inscribed in the undercroft, the building is beautifully executed; it is artfully composed as well as intensely playful; the mullions and transoms never quite meet at their intersections, leaving diagonal channels to wrap around the curved facade. It's a building worth getting up close to, not just regarding from across the street.

The deep, vertical gouge which threatened to cut Allies and Morrison's building in half has been treated in a similar manner. It has become the site for the Zig Zag, a bold, kinked urban stairway which rises to the upper level galleria, cinema, restaurants and park. Incised from the mass of the building by the masterplanners to make views of the Liver Building possible from College Lane (a move which architect Tim Makower describes as 'either unconventional or absolute genius'), the architects have made a virtue of necessity. Rising through three storeys, the architects originally imagined a long, steep, monumental flight of steps à la Montmartre. However, at a design review meeting city officials pointed out that this was Liverpool, not Paris; bars and restaurants lay at the top of the climb, not a church. Falling from top to bottom was barely worth contemplating.

this page
'There is the possibility of an
imaginative treatment to the corner',
said the brief to the architect.
The result was an act of bravado,
playfulness and whimsy.

Makower understood the point and made no attempt to sell the idea. Instead, his team began
leafing through building control diagrams and the architects discovered a rather conventional
guide to creating a cranked stair which incorporated twists and turns, as well as places for rest.
The Zig Zag, for all its eccentricity, is derived directly from that diagram. 'It's a responsive attitude
to design,' says Makower. 'A form of realism.' It was also rather bold. Escalators run beneath and the
question about whether the stair would be useful rather than merely iconic was a moot point.
The fact is, people very often choose to walk up the Zig Zag in preference to the ease of the escalator.
That people will take the harder option to better experience a building is a clear demonstration of the
power of design.

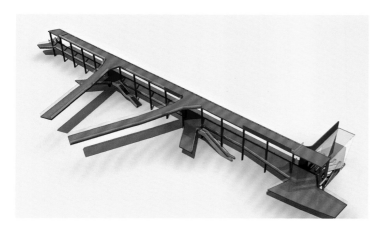
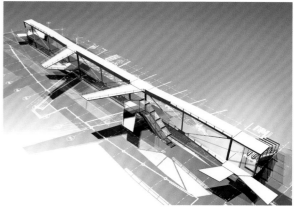

The appointment of Allies and Morrison was itself an act of faith. One of the tactics used by Grosvenor in its search for architects was to pit dependable practices with good, solid reputations against international superstars. John McAslan + Partners was lined up with Herzog & de Meuron for the design of the John Lewis store, for example. 'We had a very interesting session down in London with both practices, and it was very clear which way John Lewis wanted to go,' remembers Liverpool planning chief Michael Burchnall. McAslan's elegant analysis of both site and client need secured him the job – although the fact that he was completing a highly successful and almost total refurbishment of the Modernist Peter Jones store in London, owned by the John Lewis Partnership, did him no harm. Nonetheless, seeing off a rival bid from the global brand that is Herzog & de Meuron is no mean feat.

Allies and Morrison faced a similar heavyweight challenge, this time from Rafael Viñoly. In pitching for what was to become the Zig Zag building both firms outlined their vision to an assembly comprising Grosvenor, planning officers, ad hoc advisers and the city council's Members' Working Group, a cross-party committee that met regularly to discuss progress. 'They both made superb presentations, but Viñoly charmed the pants off everybody,' recalls Trevor Skempton, architect and urban design consultant to the city. Everybody thought the job was Viñoly's, but Rod Holmes went away, thought long and hard, and eventually appointed Allies and Morrison. The practice did not let him down and the building has received almost universal praise, partly because of the fact that it does not belong to Allies and Morrison's standard repertoire.

The case for a landmark building

In spite of the value of architectural diversity, and the alacrity with which designers were expected to respond to the project, Grosvenor always had ambitions for a landmark building. The search for coherence and contextualism was a genuine one but, all the same, Grosvenor wanted its development to be visible, not something to be encountered accidentally or by following a map. And those grand ellipses which describe the park needed, in compositional terms, a springing point. Liverpool is a city of architectural statements; there is something of a swagger about the place. The intention was never to create the sweeping grandeur and orderliness of John Nash or John Wood (both elder and younger) who redefined London and Bath during the Georgian and Regency periods. Rather, the instinct of BDP and Grosvenor was to create something of a punctuation point, performing on the skyline in much the same way as the Custom House before its post-bombing demolition. If Allies and Morrison's stone-clad behemoth was to provide the centre of gravity for the development, then something more gestural was needed to signal its

this page
The Zig Zag. This cranked stair,
the underside of which can be seen
here, negotiates the steep changes
in height across the site in the most
dramatic fashion. Such is the power of
this design, people very often take the
stair in preference to the escalator.

right

Illustration from French architects
Groupe 6, designers of the
Debenhams department store. Like
many buildings within Liverpool One,
it is a project of graceful curves –
this building, however, also performs
the role of mediating between the
traditional retail district of the city
and the many new shops within
Grosvenor's development.

In spite of the value of architectural diversity, and the alacrity with which designers were expected to respond to the project, Grosvenor always had ambitions for a landmark building

This element of Debenhams, containing the cafe which overlooks the park, has something of an early Modernist feel about it – the gentle curves, the strip windows, the striking cantilevers.

soaring ambition. The park needed framing, and views out towards the Albert Dock needed framing also. A building of some consequence was required on site 12, the triangular plot which flanks the park and the edge of the development on Strand Street.

Pelli Clarke Pelli, the Connecticut-based practice which had proved so useful in articulating the design of the park, was an obvious choice for architect. But even a firm of this international standing (this is the practice which designed Kuala Lumpur's Petronas Towers) was not immune from the almost inevitable difficulties of building high in an area of historic importance. The brief was rather vague on the matter of form other than to say that the building would be of 13 storeys at its highest point, that its park-side facade would respond to the arc of the park and that it would step down as it moved away from the waterfront. Briefly, Pelli and Grosvenor dabbled with the

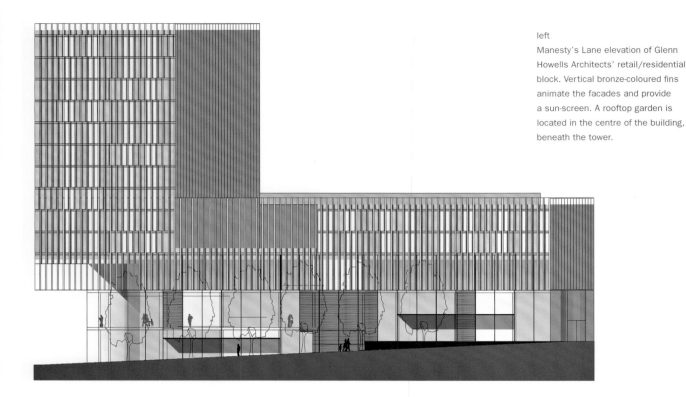

One of the tactics used
by Grosvenor in its search
for architects was to pit
dependable practices with
good, solid reputations against
international superstars

below
Elevation of Hanover Street,
illustrating how the new buildings
gradually rise to meet the height
of the elderly building on the right.
Hanover Street is deliberately a
busier, more eclectic place than
Paradise Street.

bottom left
The arcade carved through an
existing building by architects Greig &
Stephenson contains a suite of kiosks
by FAT (Fashion Architecture Taste).

bottom right
Grosvenor did not want to create a
uniformly serious and worthy estate;
rather, it aimed to inject a dose of
fun, verve and even humour.

idea of a tower approaching 40 storeys, but the city council gave the proposition short shrift. Pelli's response was something of a compromise – at 20 storeys it was half the size of that quick 'suck it and see' exercise, but half as big again as the volume agreed in the masterplan. The result was a huge difference of opinion, with Grosvenor and the City of Liverpool on the one side and conservation body English Heritage on the other.

Relations with English Heritage had always been cordial, indeed positive, over the masterplan and the height of the building that has come to be known as One Park West was the only matter that became problematic. Pelli's office cut away a large chunk of the building's mass to reduce its effect from the waterfront and create a pair of linked buildings rather than a large monolith; studies of nearby classical buildings informed the vertical and horizontal banding apparent within the facade; and diagonals were introduced to the elevation to emphasise the curve of the park. Large numbers of facade variations were tested but it all came down to the thorny issue of height, and English Heritage had a serious card to play. 'It was made very clear by English Heritage that if we pushed the Pelli scheme, they would take it through to call in,' said Liverpool's planning chief Michael Burchnall. In other words, another public inquiry, to be decided by the Secretary of State. Grosvenor had fought two public inquiries already, with all the uncertainty that went with them. A third was unconscionable.

right

Axonometric drawing of Wilkinson Eyre's car park and footbridge, shown as a kit of intersecting parts. The rectangular building at the centre is rather conventional; it is the way the circulation elements are fixed to the edges that makes this building distinctive.

below

Twisted at two key points along its length, the bridge is straight enough to provide pedestrians with an uninterrupted line-of-sight. Connecting John Lewis with a nearby car park, the department store has located large household items (such as rugs) close to the bridge entrance, allowing shoppers to transport them easily to waiting cars.

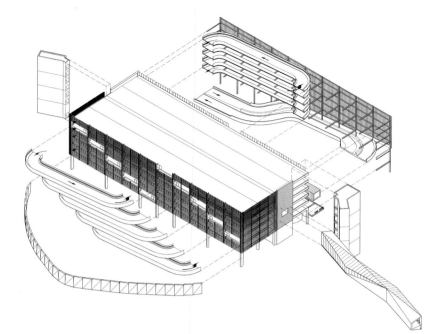

this page
Wilkinson Eyre's footbridge is a highly faceted structure, with steel plate and glazing units wrapping around this cranked tube to create a far-from-ordinary link between car park and department store. Erected in three sections, only the middle element is perpendicular to the adjacent buildings.

English Heritage's problem with height was prompted by a number of factors. The World Heritage Site listing of 2004 was uppermost in their mind, while views of the city's two cathedrals from the Albert Dock were also pertinent. Also, objectors were quick to point out that Liverpool's cluster of larger buildings was located further up the waterfront around the Three Graces – there was a general upwards sweep in the direction of the Pier Head that would be interrupted by a tall building at this particular point. 'It was too high and too dominant for that particular part of Strand Street,' said Henry Owen-John, the North-West's director for English Heritage, who admits to a 'pretty vigorous and lively debate' on the issue.

Architectural theorist Brian Hatton thinks the conservation lobby missed the point: 'Anyone who knows Liverpool knows that it's a collection of totemic objects.' Indeed. The Three Graces themselves are just such a collection. At the time of construction the Harbour Board actually objected to the height of the Liver Building, which threatened to overshadow its own spanking new headquarters; it also thought the Cunard Building should be lower. Such is the irony of heritage. Once controversial projects become cherished and ambitious new developments are curtailed (with the best of intentions) risking their own chances of attaining iconic status. The result was that Pelli's building was reduced by three storeys – not enough to affect its embrace of the park or upset the deliberate asymmetry with the lower Hilton hotel opposite, but sufficient to blunt the composition somewhat, diluting the drama of its leading edge and reining in that Liverpudlian swagger. 'It's an expressive figure that's not tall enough for its expression,' laments Brian Hatton.

Almost everyone involved found the argument over One Park West to be a difficult encounter, although the designers are surprisingly sanguine about the affair. Bill Butler, principal at Pelli

this page
One Park West by Pelli Clarke Pelli
Architects, assisted by local firm
Brock Carmichael. A landmark
building was always planned for the
western edge of Chavasse Park, but
its height proved to be a source of
controversy and argument.

Clarke Pelli Architects, says the intention was always to respond to the 'power and strength' of the Liverpool vernacular by delivering something that expressed the confidence of the city. 'Taller would have been acceptable,' he says, diplomatically. 'I don't think it would have endangered the delicacy of the site to have a building with three extra floors.' Butler argues that One Park West is not all about height – it's about the clarity of form, the rhythm of its facades, its embrace of the public realm and its role as a frame to both the park and the Mersey. When English Heritage's objections first began to filter through they were accompanied by the suggestion that the tower be merely truncated; the point of the building (in both senses of the term) would be lost. That was unacceptable to the architects, who insisted on a redesign to ensure the grand sweep of the park was terminated by a prow rather than a poop deck. 'We're very, very proud the building turned out as it did,' Butler says. 'Ultimately, you want to get something built.'

above
Liverpool One sits incredibly close
to a World Heritage Site. With
Liverpool's 'Graces' on one side,
the Rope Walks on the other, and
the Albert Dock just across the
road, the developers were never
allowed to forget the context in
which they worked.

Obsession

The One Park West episode was so maddening because Grosvenor had a heartfelt, incredibly obsessive determination to get the whole scheme right. The entire development was supposed to arrive at an equilibrium between (among other things) retail strategy, local identity, timetabling and architectural vision. It was a thoroughly thought-out, but precarious, balancing act. The development was always going to evolve, of course, and negotiations with tenants inevitably forced changes here and there. But the main issue with Cesar Pelli's building was that everyone bar English Heritage had a cast iron sense that they had cracked it, both aesthetically and commercially – unlike other buildings, such as the Hilton hotel, Grosvenor was holding on to this one and losing three storeys reduced not just the building's height but its value.

left
Spot the difference. Once
the architects had settled on the
approximate form of One Park West,
they went through almost endless
iterations on its detailing. Different
compositional arrangements
and cladding options were tried,
and the sharp inclined 'prow' of the
building was subjected to a number
of variations.

right
Although Grosvenor, the city
council and English Heritage
agreed on almost every element
of the masterplan, EH took a
different position on the height of
this building. Because of the heritage
lobby's objections, the tower was
reduced by three storeys.

'We never had an argument over the quality of materials, which was the biggest potential source of disagreement'

There is a broad consensus beyond Grosvenor that the developer's commitment to quality and 'doing the right thing' was genuine. This involved taking painful decisions. For example, Holmes was less than satisfied with BDP's treatment of the eastern corner of Lord Street and South John Street; his response was to give the facade to Marks Barfield. There was no let up. At the first sign that all was not well, Holmes would pounce. He was a demanding client and everyone, especially the architects, felt it keenly.

On the other hand, a client of such determination was a boon to designers who so often saw their designs watered down through cost control and value engineering. It was Holmes' suggestion that Allies and Morrison's building should incorporate Portland stone, a suggestion which the architects accepted gleefully. 'We never had an argument over the quality of materials, which was the biggest potential source of disagreement,' says city adviser Trevor Skempton. 'We pushed hard, but we were pushing against an open door.' This obsessiveness spread far beyond appearance and materiality; the development contains design features which are simply not apparent to the casual observer (or even the scrutiny of the critic). Studio Three's park pavilion was conceived as a pair of folded rectangles, and architect Amanda Wanner worked night and day to make sure the structure remained true to

right
South and west elevations of the pavilion. This was conceived as a 'folded' structure, created from two identical rectangles. Studio Three agonised over getting the geometry just right. They denied themselves the luxury of cheating (even if no one would notice or care).

opposite
Cut out and keep. Studio Three's demonstration of how its pavilion can be created from careful folds. Practice leader Mushtaq Saleri regularly kept two pieces of card in his pocket to demonstrate the process.

SOUTH ELEVATION

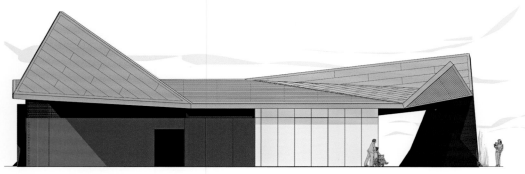

WEST ELEVATION

Liverpool is a place of hard edges and harsh weather. It's a tough place. But that doesn't mean it is immune to metaphor, symbolism or subtlety

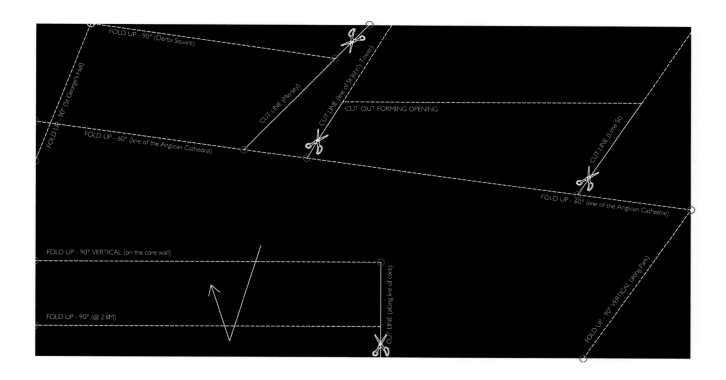

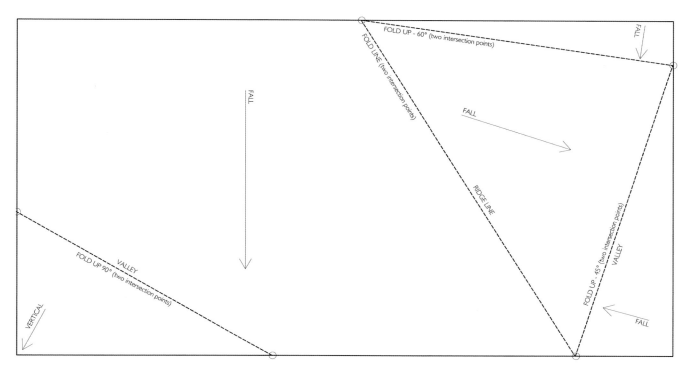

ARCHITECTURE

this page
The Hilton hotel, a collaboration
between Aedas and Squire &
Partners. Conceived as another
landmark building, the Hilton's polite
and formal composition provides a
contrast with the diagonal bravado
of One Park West.

right
The junction of Canning Place, Paradise Street and Hanover Place. Buildings converge on this site as rounded forms, partly as a response to its role as an important transport node.

this notion of pure geometry. Fudging it would have been easy, and no one would have been any the wiser. She made it work, though, and practice head Mushtaq Saleri kept two pieces of card in his breast pocket to demonstrate the solution to doubters.

below
After a competition process, Edinburgh-based firm Gross Max was selected to design the water feature on Thomas Steers Way. Landscape designers based their installation on the tidal journals of old dock harbour master William Hutchinson. Tidal measurements and the phases of the moon are traced with water jets and granite inscriptions.

Design firm Gross Max adopted a similar measure of poetry in the design of the water feature which flanks the park. Using the tidal journals of old dock harbour master William Hutchinson, who created a meticulous record of the tidal range over a period of 30 years, the practice has created a landscape of considerable intelligence. A circular pool reflects the phases of the moon while Hutchinson's tide measurements are indicated through a series of water jets. Those jets, too, mark the position of the original harbour wall. It is a multi-layered piece of design work – as simple or sophisticated as one wishes to make it. Liverpool is a place of hard edges and harsh weather; it was (perhaps it still is) an industrial-maritime city founded on both rock and commerce. It's a tough place. But that doesn't mean it is immune to metaphor, symbolism or subtlety. Liverpool thrives on this complexity, and the significance of finding a giant Liver Bird in the wreckage underneath the old Chavasse Park was lost on no one. It is these things which make a city come alive.

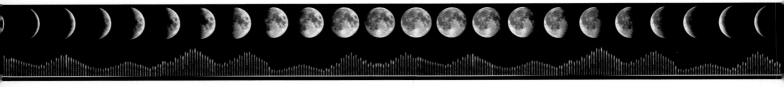

this page
Thomas Steers Way. This pedestrian
thoroughfare provides a clear link
between Liverpool's extended retail
district and the Albert Dock.

Chapter 6
DELIVERY

Chapter 6
DELIVERY

previous page
In spring 2006 Grosvenor's technical director took an important decision. Laing O'Rourke would build just the west side of the development. Balfour Beatty would build the east side, shown here.

left
The eve of opening. Although built as a single project, Liverpool One opened in two major phases, 29 May and 1 October 2008. This image, taken just prior to the first opening, illustrates the 'Sugarhouse' steps to Chavasse Park. The park itself, however, would not open until Phase Two, allowing time for the planting and newly-laid lawns to establish themselves.

The finish line

So far so good. But all the good intentions of Grosvenor's vision, its determination to aim high, would count for nothing unless the company could deliver on its promises. And Grosvenor did deliver, of course, for which it deserves considerable admiration. But it was not a hands-down victory. Completing Liverpool One so quickly and to such an exacting specification came with a price. Upon completion of this Herculean labour, Grosvenor employees were left feeling mightily proud ... if a little rueful.

It all came down to timing. On 4 June 2003 the UK government announced that Liverpool was to be the European Capital of Culture in 2008. 'Taken overall, Liverpool looked good, sounded good, feels good to be in and would deliver a really terrific year,' said Sir Jeremy Isaacs, head of the panel that made the decision. Sir David Henshaw, then the city council's chief executive, described the win as 'staggering'. What was lost amid all the excitement, however, was the fact that 42 acres of Liverpool's centre would most likely be a building site for the duration of its term as culture capital. At the time, Grosvenor was gearing up to fight a public inquiry over compulsory purchase; it didn't have the land, the designs, the builder or even the money to take its project forward. The company then did an extraordinary thing – it promised to finish its work in time for the city's big year. It was a heroic promise; and it was kept. Grosvenor was under no legal obligation to meet this new timetable. Gentle pressure was put on the project team by the city council, while some within the

company felt a sense of moral responsibility to do the best they could for Liverpool. Considering the size and complexity of the job, it was an immense achievement. Liverpool One is not just big in UK terms; it is big on a global scale and the timeframe was nothing short of punishing.

The ambitious schedule and the pace of work necessary to meet it were to prove so costly that lesser companies would have buckled under the strain. Any property development depends on finding a balance between three things: quality, time and money. Grosvenor had long wedded itself to the idea of delivering a project of the highest quality, and plenty of people were on hand to provide a constant reminder of that. Completing in time for a 2008 opening, a commitment which some came to think of as a 'moral albatross', was a matter of pride. The big question, therefore, was whether or not it was possible to bring this epic undertaking in on budget. This was no simple matter because the cost equation was linked to a wide range of factors including land values, inflation and funding arrangements; crucially, the compressed timetable meant embarking on construction before designs had been fully resolved. But, in 2004, the feeling within Grosvenor was that the company could pull it off.

Paying for it all

Underpinning the entire project was the 'development agreement', effectively the contract Grosvenor signed with the city council on 19 December 2002. The terms of this agreement specified that the project should be complete within four years of the company taking possession of the land – and the site was not fully in Grosvenor's possession until January 2005. The earliest completion date anyone could hope for was summer 2008. The development agreement did not, however, specify that building work had to start immediately – it allowed for a six month period of grace in which the company could prepare itself. But Grosvenor did not have the time to take advantage of this breathing space. If it had, Liverpool's year as European Capital of Culture would have been over by the time the project opened; importantly, this would also have dented retailers' profits, many of whom were keen to move in and start trading to take advantage of the number of visitors set to descend on the city during that year. Early completion also meant that new tenants would begin paying rent. It would be a very close run thing and Grosvenor had to act fast.

below

Contractor Laing O'Rourke began on site on the strength of its 'preferred bidder' status, which it was awarded in December 2003. A formal contract wasn't signed until much later.

Rod Holmes had written to Peter Ryan, of contractor Laing O'Rourke, as early as 19 December 2003 informing him that his company had been selected as preferred bidder for the role of 'construction partner'. So by the time that construction could actually begin towards the end of 2004, Grosvenor had just one more hurdle to overcome – raising the funds.

This might have been simpler if Henderson had still been Grosvenor's partner in Liverpool, but this firm of fund managers left the project in early 2002 because some of its bigger clients were

Archaeology

Archaeological records have long provided the people of Liverpool with a reasonable idea of what lay beneath their feet – local histories and maps were clear enough on matters such as the location of the old castle and the original wet dock, engineered by Thomas Steers. Indeed, construction in the 1960s had turned up the odd artefact; local memory and word of mouth reinforced the impression of what remained unseen. It was the detail that was lacking, though, and in spite of the fact that historians could trace very precisely the lines of the long buried wet dock, they had no idea what it was made of or how it was built – or, indeed, if it had survived at all. It was only an assumption that it had merely been filled in rather than dismantled. Archaeologists also knew that the land which wraps around the rise now topped by Derby Square was the medieval shoreline and therefore the site for ship-building and countless maritime-related activities. Apart from a relatively modest dig in the mid-1970s, prior to the building of the Queen Elizabeth II law courts, the exploration done at Liverpool One is the largest archaeological project ever undertaken in Liverpool.

Before excavating on site, Merseyside archaeological officer Sarah-Jane Farr embarked on a lengthy programme of deskwork, examining cartographic, geo-technical and historical information to establish the parameters of the study. Part of the exercise was to establish what was not known. Test investigations were first undertaken in 2001, followed by a more extensive programme three years later. Importantly, archaeologists discovered that much of the original dock walls (constructed of handmade bricks and limestone capstones) survived.

Respect for the archaeology was written into the planning process and Grosvenor was therefore obliged to investigate the archaeological potential of the site as well as 'manage, maintain and interpret' what was found. This meant preserving the dock *in situ*, rather than damaging it, so part of the foundation of the John Lewis store sits on a bridge which spans the north-east corner of the dock (although some unexpected timbers which appear to have formed some sort of strengthening role for the brickwork had to be cut away and preserved elsewhere). Also of interest was the discovery of vast sandstone blocks which architect John Foster had used to provide a foundation for the Custom House, built on top of the dock in 1828.

Archaeological investigations were not limited to the dock, however. The old Chavasse Park was also explored and the results are arguably just as enlightening as those for Canning Place. Much of the site contained rubble from the Blitz and cellars often revealed artefacts that had remained undisturbed for 60 years – including intact bottles of port. Beneath those cellars, though, were tantalising glimpses of late medieval life – fragments of 13th-century pottery, wells and boundaries. Evidence like this had been entirely absent from the city. 'It was completely unexpected that we would find evidence of settlement from this period,' says Farr.

Many of these fragments, and the remains of the dock walls, have been digitally recorded while the artefacts may form the core of a new historical collection for the city. Significantly, though, the archaeology has a more civic presence in the fabric of the Liverpool One development itself. The outline of the original dock is preserved by the rectangle traced by the rear elevations of John Lewis and the Hilton hotel, while a granite line orchestrated by landscape designers Gross Max describes the northern edge. A window has been opened up into the pavement to give passers-by a glimpse of the preserved dock wall. The route between the hotel and the park, originally conceived as a 'discovery axis', has been named Thomas Steers Way.

Liverpool One   Remaking a city centre

beginning to withdraw from retail developments. Undaunted, Grosvenor pursued a twin-track approach in the search for partners – it would look for both loans and investors. Originally, the development was projected to cost £650 million and the company eventually put together a package comprising £255 million of equity (in which Grosvenor itself has a 20 per cent stake) and £400 million of debt, financed by four banks (see Appendix B). The bank loans were secured relatively easily, but the terms of the equity holders (partners in what came to be known as the Grosvenor Liverpool Fund) were far more demanding. Although Grosvenor had a stake in the fund, the remaining contributors decided that investment vehicle Hermes should represent them in negotiations. And Hermes drove a very hard bargain indeed. The upshot was that investors said there would be a limit to their investment; apart from a contingency fund of £50 million, any cost overruns would have to be borne by Grosvenor alone. 'This cost cap hurt Grosvenor the most,' according to John Irvine, Grosvenor's development director for projects outside London. Hermes was in the enviable position of being able to comment on materials and quality thresholds without having to bear the burden of the extra cost. This was hardly a cynical move, though; Hermes et al were anxious to protect their clients' investments and they had also committed to a very long-term partnership. No one insisted on getting their money back upon completion – these investors, like Grosvenor, were in it for the long haul. Even so, it seems Grosvenor found itself in an awkward position and it had few options. The only plausible alternative was to walk away and begin building on the strength of the bank loans and Grosvenor's own resources, returning to the negotiating table when there was more certainty (and less risk) associated with the project. This option was fully explored at board level and it was decided, probably rightly, that going it alone was not a viable course of action; even for Grosvenor the sums involved would have been too large for a single project and may well have forced cuts in other parts of the business. So by the end of 2004, Grosvenor had a funding deal on offer. The terms were harsh, but it was funding.

above
The creation of Pelli Clarke Pelli
Architects' One Park West building
was Grosvenor's most significant
contribution to Liverpool's changing
skyline. Apartments in this
residential building were sold in
phases; 25 units were sold in a
matter of hours; four of the larger
apartments were sold within 10
minutes of being put on the market.

Project management

At the time, Grosvenor genuinely believed it could manage the project on these strict terms; directors knew there was financial risk involved, but it was a calculated risk borne aloft by a sense of optimism and a determination to demonstrate that the company could deliver a city centre every bit as good as its Georgian forebears. As it turned out, however, this project took place against a background of rapidly rising property prices and rampant inflation in the construction sector. And when Laing O'Rourke began building in earnest, designs had yet to be fully resolved. Pinning down a build price was difficult, especially when designs continued to evolve (the cinema building, for example, almost doubled in size). At first, the project team tried to incentivise the contractor by proposing to share both savings and overruns – if tendering could establish a base price for a particular portion of work, the contractor would take half of any savings made but bear the burden of half of any excess too. 'At the outset Grosvenor was mindful of the fact that nearly all major projects in the UK over-run financially. We were determined to avoid that situation if at all possible. We looked at different forms of procurement and discussed them widely throughout the industry,' says Rod Holmes. The incentive formula was well intended, and it even had one or two early successes before breaking down due to the insufficient level of design detail and the construction

Rod Holmes

During a visit from their native Connecticut, to conduct a site tour of their One Park West building, PCPA architects Bill Butler and Fred Clarke took a walk around the rest of the emerging development. Turning down College Lane they spotted a pair of street cleaners with 'The Rod Squad' emblazoned on the back of their hi-viz jackets. The cleaners knew Rod Holmes, it turned out, and they explained to the architects that he took a keen interest in the work of everybody on the development: all involved were left with a clear impression that they were a small but vital part of a wider project. When the maker of the 1:500 model on display in the Liverpool One information office had a question, he would call Rod Holmes personally.

Holmes has been called a control freak more than once. 'He's almost unique because of the sheer breadth and drive of his involvement,' says BDP masterplanner Terry Davenport. This is why Holmes was appointed to the project in the first place – to live and breathe it, to obsess about it and push people hard. 'There was no magic – just a lot of highly motivated people with one very strong leader,' says technical director Bill Allen, who sees the stability of the project team as one of the principal achievements of Grosvenor's endeavour in the city. 'It's a psychological effort. A lot of people assume that happens naturally. It doesn't. You have to work at it.'

A Yorkshireman who has now made Liverpool his adopted home, Holmes is a man who likes to be sure of his facts; if anyone is to cross or contradict him, Holmes will listen carefully to a persuasive argument and quickly see through bluff and excuses. But no one can press a

project as political and sensitive as Liverpool One through to completion without a certain degree of charm. Chamber of Commerce chief executive Jack Stopforth remembers Holmes for his technical insight, but adds that he was always brave enough to tell the truth as he saw it while being diplomatic enough to get away with it. 'Rod would stand up

in front of Liverpool City Council and tell them their streets were a disgrace. He would get straight to the point, but in a very engaging way.'

'The whole project has proceeded on Rod's ability to carry people with him,' says Guy Butler, who took over from Holmes as project director on 1 October 2008.

industry's diminishing appetite for risk at the time. In fact, Laing O'Rourke was at a fairly advanced
stage of construction before a contract was finally signed; the company had begun on site merely
on the strength of its 'preferred bidder' status, and lengthy negotiations on the final terms of the
contract were concluded only after law firm Linklaters was brought in to sort things out. 'This
whole period was very stressful', admits Holmes.

Clearly, being in possession of both land and funding did not mean that construction would be
plain sailing. Managing the build process involved an almost constant round of tough decisions,
and Rod Holmes wasn't the only person making them. Bill Allen, who joined the team from
Hammerson after working on the reinvention of Birmingham's Bull Ring, was the delivery team's
technical director. He was also a tough player. While there was no element of the wider programme
in which Rod Holmes didn't take a keen interest (aesthetic, political, commercial, legal), it was
Allen's job to keep pressing relentlessly to the finish line. He was often present at regular 'super-
crits' when architects and council officials would meet to chew over building details, refining,
improving, commenting, cajoling and even sending designers away with their tails between their
legs. 'There can't be endless iterations. The design phase has to be effective and smooth', says
Allen. 'I think I was the project's practical conscience. People thought "Oh no, who let him in the

this page
Street entertainers celebrated
the opening of Liverpool One. On
1 October 2008, fireworks were
launched from the roofs of One
Park West and the Hilton hotel.

room?''. The reason for Allen's concern was not just that matter of scale: delivering a large project is one thing, but this was not a virgin site; there was precious archaeology beneath the builders' feet, as well as Victorian vaults. And then there was the danger of unexploded Luftwaffe bombs and uncertainty about the porosity of the ground – the last thing Grosvenor needed was for deep excavations to fill with water from the Mersey. Mercifully, after tiptoeing around the site, probing (expensively) here and there, no bombs were found. Ground conditions turned out to be very good, although there were more electrical and fibre optic cables than the builders had bargained for.

Worse, the timetable was in danger of slipping. Laing O'Rourke had been commissioned on the broad understanding that it would build the entire development, but for the first year of construction the area to the west of Paradise Street had been the focus of everyone's attention; a good deal of the east was being neglected. In the spring of 2006 Bill Allen took an important decision; Laing O'Rourke, he felt, did not have the capacity to deliver the entire project on time and he proposed to find another contractor for the east side of the site. Laing O'Rourke protested loudly; they had, after all, already delivered the Wilkinson Eyre-design bus station and six-storey car park (which went on to win an award from the Royal Institute of British Architects). But Allen stuck to his guns and the rest of Grosvenor backed him. 'I joined in the full knowledge that 2008 was sacrosanct,' remembers Allen. 'It was a very hard decision. And from a Grosvenor project manager point of view, it put even more stress on our guys.' No longer would all construction documentation be channelled to a single point of contact, and now the project team would have to manage the boundary which separated the two contractors, ensuring that everything joined neatly.

The search for a second builder ended with the selection of Balfour Beatty which built (along with its subsidiaries Mansell and Birse Group) Dixon Jones' Peter's Lane arcade, the Haworth Tompkins buildings and Glenn Howells' tower, among other things.

It was a testing time. Quite apart from the pressure of resolving issues with contractors, the project team found itself mired in bureaucracy. More than half a million pages of documentation had been amassed and Grosvenor's insistence on keeping a hard copy of everything meant that a suite of rooms had to be made available to contain it all. Rod Holmes was becoming frustrated and he complained to the local press that the paperwork was threatening to steer the project off course. But red tape was proving to be the least of the team's worries; costs continued to rise. Rod Holmes looked for savings where he could, and became fiercely indignant whenever accused of 'value engineering' – value for money, yes, but reducing quality in the name of economy was not on the agenda. Rod Holmes remembers Stephen Musgrave, then chief executive of Grosvenor Great Britain & Ireland, telling him not to 'dumb it down' and deliver what was promised: 'But we had to keep revisiting the designs as they were being built. We therefore had to keep renegotiating the price.'

Commenting on the 'huge timetable and financial pressures' facing the company, Holmes told the *Liverpool Daily Post* in January 2006 that Grosvenor would deliver the project as promised. 'There is always the risk, under such circumstances, that it could lead to a dumbing down of the vision. Grosvenor is determined to make sure that this does not happen, partly because of its commitments to its partners and the people of Merseyside; and partly because it is a commercial imperative – unless the project delivers something very special, as the single biggest component of the new Liverpool, it will not achieve the financial returns that are required to justify the huge investment. The entire team working on the project knows there is no turning back.'

In the summer of that year Grosvenor's chief executive for Great Britain and Ireland, Stephen Musgrave, departed to head up the UK arm of property firm Hines. Mark Preston, who had spent four years as president of Grosvenor USA, replaced him. Preston had long been aware that

Delivering a large project is one thing, but this was not a virgin site; there was precious archaeology beneath the builders' feet

this page
Inside the old dock. Before
Grosvenor's development of the
site, archaeologists had little idea of
the construction of Thomas Steers'
structure, completed in 1715.

Liverpool was costing more than envisaged, and he was determined to seek some clarity. 'I didn't know how big it was, but I knew there was a hole opening up,' says Preston. The day he started in his new job, Preston promoted John Irvine to the role of development director for projects outside London, and the pair of them began to subject the cost of Liverpool One to the closest scrutiny. This new top team brought a certain freshness to the project – they had no preconceptions, they could ask whatever they liked, and they gave everyone else a licence to speak plainly. 'It was essential the team knew that messengers would not be shot,' recalls Preston. The result of this inquiry was surprising and alarming. Early findings indicated that rising land values (which forced up the cost of acquiring the site) and spiralling construction costs had led to an overrun of at least £90 million, and very probably a great deal more. In April 2007, Grosvenor announced that its project in Liverpool had lost the company £150 million.

Clearly, tough new control measures were in order. Organisational structures were tightened; Preston made the project management director, Steve Brewer, directly responsible to him. Preston also began to chair the Liverpool steering group; this committee, set up to provide oversight for

previous page
Clearly visible from the Odeon's bar, the roofscape of the adjacent mixed-use building has been neatly arranged to make the service and ventilation kit a thing of utilitarian beauty.

right
Throughout the lifetime of the project, Grosvenor was determined to keep quality thresholds high. Street furniture is slick and exemplary; stone, rather than being applied as thin wafers, is solid.

below right
Liverpool One is a retail-led scheme, not a retail-only development. If it was about shops and little else, Grosvenor would not have built a 5 acre park. The park does, however, create a sense of place that is attractive to families – and that will, of course, have a positive effect on retailers.

above

The facade of One Park West.
The mullions have been designed
at a rakish angle to emphasise the
curve of the building. When viewed
from the adjacent park, the building
appears almost convex.

above right

This is one of the very few covered
escalators in Liverpool One.
Escalators are unusual features
in an external urban setting, and
the architects originally considered
providing canopies for each one. They
thought better of it – such weather
protection was considered to be
unnecessary and visually intrusive.

the project, was also strengthened through the appointment of former Hammerson chairman the late Ron Spinney, a widely respected and insightful industry figure. (His position on the steering committee was taken by Michael Gradon, a non-executive director of Grosvenor and a former director of P & O.) Costs continued to be challenged directly. A commitment to quality was always maintained, however, and value engineering never appeared on the agenda. Consequently, the delivery team had to take a long, hard look at what it had planned and make some tough choices: if quality could not be sacrificed in the name of cost-saving, then some elements within the wider project would have to go. One of the pavilions envisaged for the park, designed by Glenn Howells, was cancelled. In spite of the company's determination to get a firm grip on cost control, insiders began to fear that the gloom would spread to the delivery team and cause such a loss of confidence that people would begin to leave. They didn't. 'The commitment of the team was fantastic,' says John Irvine. Also, retail strategists became anxious that potential tenants would come to think that making a loss was somehow symptomatic of trying to do business in Liverpool. That didn't happen either.

Grosvenor had found itself torn between its commitments to quality and timeliness, and the commercial necessity of financial prudence. Slowly but surely, being seen to deliver on its promises became the dominant factor, in spite of the financial pain. What became apparent during Mark Preston's review was that, apart from the under-estimate of the price of the project at the very start, there was no single moment which steered costs off course; rather, it was a very slow, incremental process. Jeremy Newsum, then group chief executive and now executive trustee and a non-executive director of the group board, gives this honest assessment: 'Everybody has some culpability somewhere. There was a clear failure of the board to make the right decisions, as well as the failures of individuals. The board failed to expose the weaknesses within the management team in good time.' In fairness to Grosvenor, which can afford to be rather hard on itself now that the dust has settled and the development is completed, it was not as if the complexities of the project were ignored. Rather, the qualities of trust, dependability and determination to deliver as promised are so deeply impregnated within the corporate culture that there seemed to be no other way of doing things. Grosvenor has emerged with its brand intact, as well as a project which is perceived as *the* way to redevelop a city centre.

this page
Between John Lewis and the
steps to the park is a small window,
through which Thomas Steers' dock
can be seen.

The arrival of Liverpool One was a transformational moment for the city, but merely the opening chapter on a narrative that has a long way to run. It would be inappropriate to judge Grosvenor or Liverpool One on an early evaluation of its success – commercial or otherwise. Liverpool One is a long-term bet and Grosvenor, with its long-term perspective, can afford to wait for the payback.

Open for business

Liverpool One was too big to hold everything back until a state of total completion had been achieved. Key streets had to open as early as possible to relieve the pressure of people visiting for the big Capital of Culture events. Retailers wanted to open for business, for a start, while there was a general clamour and impatience among the public to be allowed back in – even if just for curiosity's sake. The bus station and adjacent car park were opened in November 2005, while the BBC and 'Bling Bling' buildings took shape the following year and were also early openers. The bulk of the estate to the west of Paradise Street was inaugurated in one fell swoop on 29 May 2008, when thousands of people pressed into South John Street en masse and the front page of the *Liverpool Echo* ran the headline 'Open ... All Ours'. Just four months later, on 1 October, the rest of the development, including the eagerly awaited Chavasse Park, opened. The Princess Royal unveiled a plaque and the Duke of Westminster, speaking against driving rain on the steps of the park, thanked the people of the city for their patience. The project was, said the Duke, 'a tour de force, involving many people and lots of effort'. Indeed.

Watching the response of those who had turned out on that wet Wednesday afternoon was fascinating. They tested its permeability, weaving their way from Church Street, via the new arcades, to the terrace of restaurants overlooking the park and the Mersey – not because they needed to, but because they *could*. It was still identifiably their city; the street pattern and views were much the same. They knew where they were, and where they were going, but it was an adventure all the same. What is more, the predictions of the architects were proved right: the Peter's Lane arcade really was illuminated with a wash of light, even when cloud obscured the sun; glimpses of the Liver Building really were provided by the clever little slots and cuts contained within the masterplan; it felt not remotely like a faceless shopping mall. At the time, not everything was done and dusted. Some of the older buildings along Hanover Street were still in the process of being rescued from the ravages of age. Towards the Rope Walks one or two buildings were awaiting demolition in order for Liverpool One to extend its power for renewal

Liverpool One is a long-term bet and Grosvenor, with its long-term perspective, can afford to wait for the payback

deeper into the city. And then there were the buildings which sit outside the core 'funded scheme' which would not open until the following spring – notably the £60 million Hilton hotel and the £80 million One Park West complex, which Grosvenor financed itself. When all the numbers are added up, it really is a £1 billion project. 'No one apart from Grosvenor could have delivered this project,' says John Bullough, now chief executive officer at property firm Aldar. 'We would never stop, never give up. It was a matter of pride that Grosvenor would deliver. That was the mindset. These values are deeply engrained.'

Locals, both officials and the wider population, couldn't quite believe what had happened. The Paradise Street/Chavasse Park area had gone undeveloped for so long that it was difficult for anyone to believe that change would eventually happen, especially on such a vast scale. The sense of mission accomplished was profound. 'Anywhere else outside China it would have taken 15 years. But we did it,' says former city council leader Mike Storey. His successor, Warren Bradley, speaking at a champagne reception on the evening of 1 October, offered this succinct appraisal: 'Liverpool is back. And it's because of people like Grosvenor.'

Chapter 7
REFLECTIONS

Chapter 7
REFLECTIONS

previous page
Many remained sceptical about
what could be achieved in Liverpool,
in spite of the figures that showed
the city was gradually recovering.
Liverpool One had to be built with
the glue of faith.

left
Liverpool One is about more
than shops – people live here too.
These apartments, which share
a raised courtyard, look out over
Paradise Street.

From start to finish in a decade. For any inner city development of this scale, that timetable is nothing short of impressive; for a development of this quality, the achievement is no less than outstanding. Much of the raw material was promising in the first place: a visionary city council; a broad commitment to partnership; a developer with a long-term perspective and an almost moral sense of duty and integrity; a first rate masterplan underpinned by very human values. And yet an awful lot was lined up against the project. There was a cynicism, born of stereotyping, about what could be achieved in Liverpool. The expectations of retailers, on which the entire success of the project is predicated, might have prised the principles of this vision apart; this is a sector which has such a deep sense of 'what the customer wants' that variations on a theme, and wholesale reinvention, are met with a certain suspicion. The openness with which Grosvenor dealt with stakeholders and other interested parties could so easily have led to design by committee. For all the financial planning and policy-making, Liverpool One is a project that has been pieced together, bit by bit, with the glue of faith.

Between 1998 and 2006 the number of people employed in Liverpool rose by 12 per cent, a figure which exceeds most other comparable cities. The number of businesses in the 'knowledge economy' sector also rose by more than the national average. But back in the late 1990s figures like these were mere predictions. There was a general consensus that Liverpool's fortunes were on the rise, but the most convincing case the city could make was one of potential. Its heritage, its energy, the new

right
'Liverpool One is a substantial achievement: the most persuasive city-centre redevelopment that has been completed in Britain for many years,' wrote Ellis Woodman in architects' magazine *Building Design*. 'The mix of uses, the relatively modest scale of the urban blocks and the range of authorship are exemplary, and while it could hardly be opening in a less sympathetic economic climate, one wishes it every luck.' Debenhams department store, South John Street.

below
Grosvenor and its architects were not afraid of counterpointing Liverpool's historic buildings with contemporary design. 'Pastiche' is not in Grosvenor's vocabulary.

political landscape, the willingness to embrace the private sector, the sense of determination – the city was certainly facing in the right direction, but everyone involved in building a new city centre had to become an evangelist. This was to be no ordinary job.

This is why the personalities at the heart of this epic project are so important. To get it moving there needed to be people of considerable drive and passion behind the job titles. There could be no hedging of bets or get-out clauses and the city council was exceptionally shrewd to draw up a development agreement that included no mention of commercial viability. The agreement which bound Grosvenor to the project specified that building work had to commence once four things had been achieved: that anchor tenants had been secured; that the CPO process had been concluded satisfactorily; that a road closure order had been obtained; and that planning permission was granted. Normally, these contracts also include something to the effect that the development has to be commercially viable (a clause which is now found in all of Grosvenor's development agreements). This one didn't. If it had, Grosvenor would have had a chance to walk away, or at least buy more time. As it was, Grosvenor took the plunge right at the beginning. There was no escape route or Plan B. This was to prove costly in financial terms, but it forced a degree of resolve on the company that ensured a complex, gigantic and high quality project was brought in on time. This is virtually unheard of in the Western world. 'If we'd got any other developer here, we probably would not have got this scheme completed,' says the city council's Michael Burchnall.

The city council had always aimed for something big, daring and transformational. Too often they'd tried more discreet improvements which had met with only partial success because they lacked the critical mass to shift the entire city up a gear. This was different, of another order entirely; it was a project that needed strong, visionary leadership and a thoroughly business-like approach. To reinvent the city, the council first needed to reinvent itself. Council leader Mike Storey and chief executive Sir David Henshaw deserve much recognition for this reinvention; unfortunately, both resigned their posts three years before Liverpool One was completed, but after sufficient tenure to give the project the momentum it needed in its early phases. Officials knew they could not just bring in a developer and let them get on with it, watching from the perimeter fence and lobbing over obstacles when it suited them. They had to be involved. 'The processes the city council has gone through to get to where they are with Liverpool One have been invaluable, not just in demonstrating that Liverpool is a city with which one can do business, but one where the council as a partner can deliver,' wrote the city council's former regeneration chief Charlie Parker in 2006.

When Grosvenor settled a finance package with the equity holders, the company took a huge financial risk; as costs rose, the directors' determination to deliver as promised grew too. Grosvenor's job now, internally, is to learn from its mistakes and recalibrate the balance between honour and financial success. 'Trust' is one of the company's core values that is quite simply non-negotiable; profit and cost-control are similarly fundamental to commercial success and senior staff are adamant that the development business will not rely on assets held elsewhere in the group

below
The department store (right) and retail/residential block (left) are different but complementary pieces of architecture.

to fill troublesome gaps on the balance sheet. In the future, clients can fully expect Grosvenor to mix more financial grit with that aura of dependability. 'I'm quite clear that, going forward, if we don't get the right terms in development agreements, we just won't do it,' says John Irvine. Irvine will also be looking for more flexibility in these contracts, including the timing of delivery, to give the company a little room for manoeuvre. In fact, by common consent the company should have delayed going on site for a whole year to allow for more design certainty. There is also the sobering thought that if Grosvenor had acted a little more cautiously, Liverpool One would have been completed just in time for an economic downturn to scare retailers witless. Then there would have been trouble. Getting caught up with Capital of Culture fever and pressing relentlessly on to a 2008 finish was, perhaps, not such a bad thing after all.

For all those involved in the project, it is regrettable that the satisfaction of completing something so big and rejuvenating has to be counterbalanced with lessons learned. There is some solace to be found in the fact that ambitious property developments can never happen without something, somewhere, going wrong. But senior managers within the company are determined to learn from Liverpool, no matter how uncomfortable or awkward the lesson. One significant change within Grosvenor Great Britain & Ireland has been the separation of the roles of chief executive and development director, which were combined until 2006. At the same time, the development teams responsible for strategically guiding projects, and the project management teams given the job of actually building them, were made separately accountable to the company board. In Liverpool the line between these two activities was blurred, to say the least.

Liverpool One is the largest city centre regeneration project to have been undertaken in the UK for a very long time and something of this scale is unlikely to come up again for another generation. That might well apply to the rest of Europe, too. The eyes of the property community are upon the project, looking to see what happens when a developer reinvents a city centre so comprehensively – not with the reformist arrogance of the postwar era but with the confidence that springs from

this page
Liverpool City Council commissioned
Grosvenor to deliver something
transformational. In spite of the
financial and timetabling difficulties
encountered during this project, the
property developer did exactly that.

Grosvenor has emerged strong, focused and better organised. The company continues to hold on to its values of openness and transparency

left
Grosvenor often talks about 'living cities'. This is one definition of that term: urban spaces that provide a frame and reference point in which people can live their lives. Humour and quirkiness are definitely allowed.

right
The original dock which put Liverpool on the path to success had disappeared from memory and view. This development, through public art and landscaping, reminds Liverpudlians of the importance of that lost piece of maritime infrastructure.

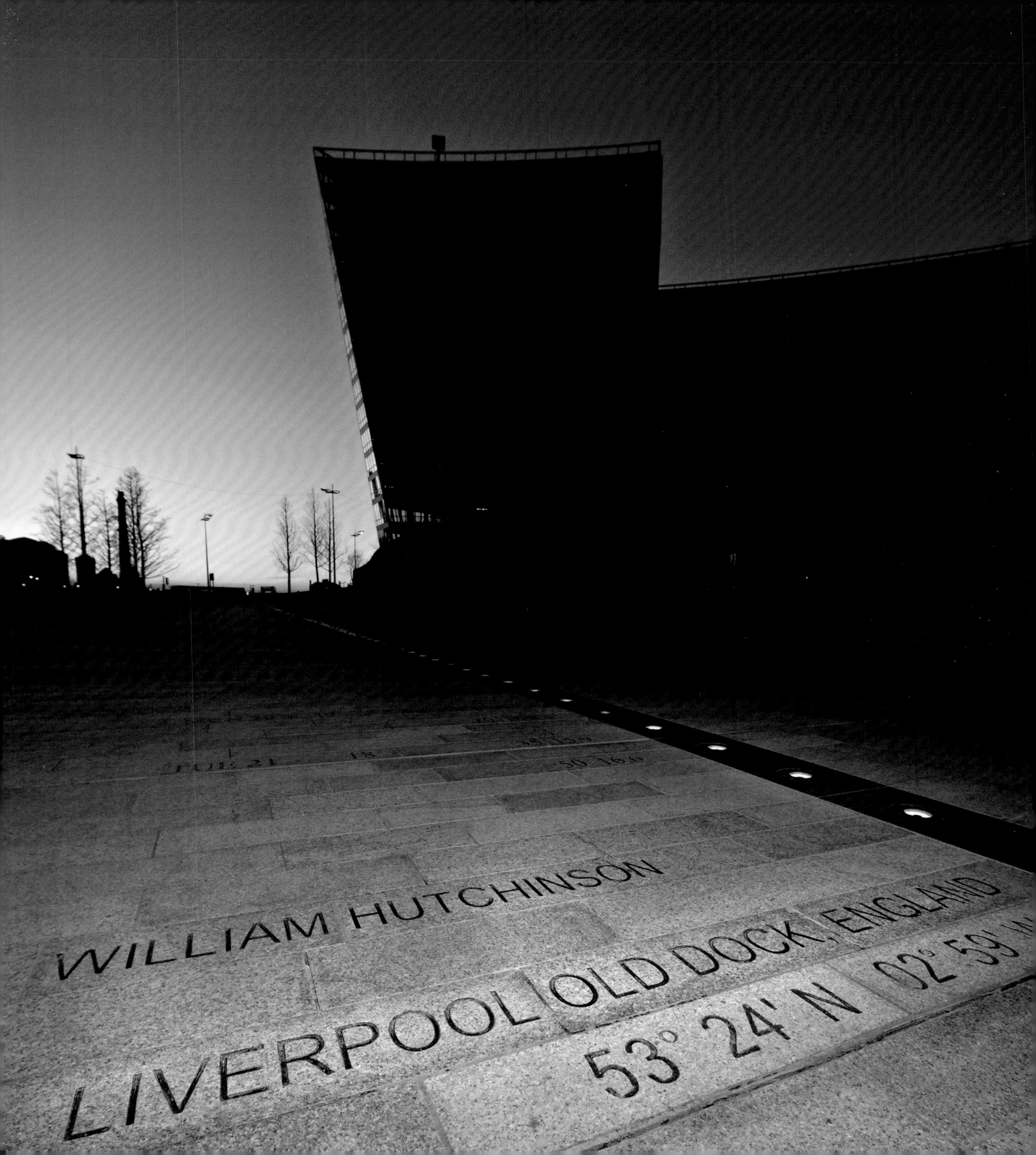
WILLIAM HUTCHINSON
LIVERPOOL OLD DOCK, ENGLAND
53° 24' N
02° 59'

this page
One Park West and the Hilton hold
the renewed Chavasse Park in
their embrace. In spite of English
Heritage's demands that the
residential tower be shortened,
architect Bill Butler says he bears
no grudge.

understanding what goes into making a place where people genuinely like to be. There is no doubt that other cities will eventually follow suit, albeit in more modest ways. Mark Preston, now Grosvenor's group chief executive, has an interesting perspective on all that has been learned in Liverpool: 'This is the ideal way to deliver this kind of regeneration. I don't think you'll find anyone who is critical of what we've produced. But we won't do it this way again; probably nobody else will either.' What he means is that quickly redeveloping a large, inner city, brownfield site in one fell swoop (especially one that is built to last) is just too complex. Projects like this will, in future, be delivered in two or more phases, and artificial deadlines to suit the needs of others (no matter how noble) are unlikely to cut much ice in the Grosvenor boardroom. It is a shame, of course. Everybody likes big, dramatic gestures, especially ones that turn a vision into reality within the blink of an eye. But Grosvenor is now considerably more streetwise than it was in its pre-Liverpool days; a little less heroic, a bit less reliant on instinct, a touch more calculating. Future partners of Grosvenor will notice the company taking a more prudent approach to control and risk.

For all its losses, Grosvenor has emerged strong, focused and better organised. The company continues to hold on to its values of openness and transparency. Being a private company, Grosvenor is not obliged to make its accounts public, but it chooses to do so. Directors could very easily wrap their business in a veil of secrecy; cost and accounting matters could be considered a private affair and bad news left merely to rumour and dinner party gossip. But an approach of this sort would be counter to the spirit of openness and partnership with which Grosvenor likes to conduct its affairs.

Grosvenor is attracted to partnership agreements almost instinctively. That is why it was appointed by Liverpool City Council in the first place. The city's officials and elected members were impressed that Grosvenor never pretended to have all the answers; equally, the idea that 'we're all in this together' was impressive. The developer saw itself as part of an extended team and took great satisfaction in tackling a monumental problem as a shared endeavour. Liverpool City Council not only got a world class retail heart which stitched the city back together after half a century of mismanagement, but it got 5,000 full time jobs, a massive boost to business rates (due to the new businesses operating there) and a substantial ground rent. All in return for granting a 250-year lease for the site. The boost that Liverpool One has given to the local and regional economy should not be underestimated.

So what did Grosvenor get? Well, it got a number of things. The company got the chance to prove that it could deliver a technically challenging, first rate city centre to the satisfaction of everyone involved. It has demonstrated what intelligent urban regeneration can look like. The company has been able to prove that its brand values of trust, dependability and competence actually count for something. It has amassed knowledge and experience that will (assuming the lessons fully embed themselves in corporate culture) benefit the company for a generation. Grosvenor also got itself another long-term asset. True, it doesn't own that asset outright, but the company owns enough of it to be valuable in the long run. And managers of the Grosvenor Liverpool Fund are not going to sit back and idly wait for the development to pay for itself; they are actively nurturing this estate and will add (and extract) value whenever the opportunity presents itself. The estate may even expand. 'I'm convinced Grosvenor will find ways in the future to generate more value from what they've created,' says Mervyn Howard, the company's UK fund management director.

Howard is also convinced that the departure of Henderson from the development team made very little difference to the final outcome. It would be easy to pin much of the blame for Grosvenor's financial difficulties with Liverpool One on the fund manager's decision to quit the project in 2002. It was Henderson, after all, whose job it was to raise the money for the project; with such

a key partner missing, was Grosvenor not at a disadvantage? That, surely, would go some way to explaining the tough terms on which the developer eventually managed to find investors? Not really. Howard believes the terms on which Grosvenor brought in investors wouldn't be much different if they'd been negotiated by Henderson. And the approach the equity partners brought to the negotiating table had little or nothing to do with Grosvenor's vulnerability; rather, it had everything to do with the fact that they were being asked to back a scheme which had yet to be designed. Moreover, close to the point at which a deal was to be signed, the delivery team increased the forecast cost of the project. That unsettled everybody. Hermes and the others can hardly be blamed for placing a limit on their investments. It is not the role of investors to feel the pleasure and excitement of a job well done; theirs is merely to pay for it and seek a financial return.

Grosvenor's views on what makes a city live, breathe and come alive remain unchanged, though. Aside from the commercial and corporate governance issues which the project threw up, Liverpool One is Grosvenor's most complete example of how to approach urban renewal. The result is a new slice of city founded not on architecture but on masterplanning, place-making, diversity and local identity. True, the architecture is important, but the architecture is merely the flesh on the

right
Terry Davenport, BDP architect.
His flare for masterplanning, as
well as his local knowledge, was
instrumental in the success of
this development.

bones of a masterplan that arose out of a profound sympathy with the city of Liverpool. Grosvenor can take a lot of credit for the advent of that masterplan, but so too should the BDP team led by Terry Davenport, a local man whose familiarity with the city gave the approach a rapid dose of authenticity that would otherwise have taken much longer to fathom. It is this 'v' view that has enabled the development to be so quickly accepted; those views of key historic buildings are not all brand new – they have simply been preserved and reframed. The development team was able to tap into what Liverpudlians wanted to look at, how they saw their city and how they wanted others to see it and negotiate it.

'Everybody is quite blown away by it, and I don't think you'll find anyone locally with any real quibbles,' says John Stonard, the programme manager at the Commission for Architecture and the Built Environment. 'I'm a Liverpudlian. I've seen schemes come and go for this site. The important thing for me is how the city has been knitted back together. It's incredibly successful. The huge achievement is in the place-making. Compare this with what could have been built, or is being built around the country. This is a major step forward.'

In presentational terms Liverpool One is a retail-led, mixed-use development. That is a phrase that falls pitifully short of the ways in which people are experiencing this rejuvenated, repaired city centre. It is now a piece of urban life and is therefore not a finished solution to Liverpool's problems but a growing, organic, ever-changing and highly adaptable streetscape. The project is one of spaces and the relationships between them, populated by buildings. As a piece of modern city, this estate will inevitably change. Some buildings will surely be replaced; some may become cherished and protected by the embrace of English Heritage; the balance of traffic and pedestrians may alter; and the character of places may adjust itself as the fashions and tastes of clientele shift over time. That is as it should be, and the masterplan (which is what all this is about) will not only survive the winds of change but may well facilitate them. It is strong and intelligent enough. This is one of the consequences of Grosvenor's commitment to 'living cities'; that the agents of progress, provided they are sufficiently robust and meaningful, can themselves be the subject of change. Just look at Mayfair and Belgravia; these estates have managed an effortless response to three centuries of transformation while preserving the principles that underwrote them in the first place. That is the real purpose of the masterplan described in this book, to provide a foundation on which Liverpool can usefully move forward. What Grosvenor has done is help put Liverpool back on its feet. Not only that, they put a spring in its step.

this page
'Grosvenor's embrace of the best
of the best would scare a lesser
company. However, its vision will
undoubtedly underpin Liverpool's
long-term future,' wrote Fiona
Hamilton in *Property Week*. 'This
project has given – to a once-dejected
cityscape – something genuinely
enhancing and uplifting that will
inspire people's day-to-day lives.'

Appendix A
TIMELINE

The following is a list of key dates in the formulation of postwar urban policy in Liverpool, and important moments in the development of Liverpool One.

1958
Development plan for Liverpool formulated.

1965
City centre plan drawn up, including a comprehensive redevelopment area for Strand Street and Paradise Street.

1981
Merseyside Development Corporation (MDC) formed as planning authority;

October, strategic guidance for Merseyside (PPG 11) issued, recognising Liverpool as a key regional centre and specifying that retail provision be located in town centres. Reiterated by guidance in 1996.

1988
MDC becomes the planning authority for an extended area of city centre.

1990
Pieda commissioned by MDC to undertake City Centre Retail Study.

1993
City Centre Plan published by Liverpool City Council and MDC;

July, Merseyside accorded Objective 1 status by EU.

1995
March, Liverpool City Council begins to draw up a list of 'ambitions' and a 'vision' for the city with focus groups.

1996
April, deposit draft Unitary Development Plan (UDP) approved by city council.

1997
City council publishes influential *Ambitions for the City* document.

1998
March, MDC is wound up;

June, Healey & Baker appointed by city council to conduct retail study.

1999
February, Healey & Baker issues retail study;

2 March, retail study adopted by city council as formal strategy, forming the basis of Paradise Street Development Area (PSDA) planning framework;

5 June, advertisements placed in *Financial Times* and *Estates Gazette* calling for developers' interest in redeveloping the PSDA;

18 June, deadline for developers to register interest in PSDA;

June, development agency Liverpool Vision established, comprising the Northwest Regional Development Agency, Liverpool City Council, English Partnerships and the private sector;

2 August, questionnaire issued to interested developers;

October, PSDA outline development brief drawn up by city council and Healey & Baker;

4 October, developer shortlist drawn up;

22 October, outline development brief issued to shortlisted companies;

17 December, shortlisted developers submit written responses to outline development brief.

2000
11 to 14 January, workshops with shortlisted companies;

8 to 9 February, shortlisted companies make formal presentations to the city council;

6 March, Grosvenor Henderson selected;

May, consultation exercise launched into the PSDA planning framework. 325 copies sent out for consultation;

July, Liverpool Vision issues *Strategic Regeneration Framework*, identifying PSDA as central to plan to develop city's retail sector;

November, city council issues Grosvenor with final development brief.

2001
17 January, masterplan submitted for planning;

May, public exhibition of proposals;

October, planning application amended to take account of comments from consultations;

4 November, public inquiry into amending the city's Unitary Development Plan to include the plans for the PSDA.

2002

22 February, conclusion of public inquiry into UDP;

8 May, public inquiry inspector publishes report accepting case for modifying the UDP;

2 July, inquiry inspector finds in favour of Grosvenor and city council, dismissing rival claims to develop Chavasse Park by Walton Group;

4 September, revised UDP formally adopted by city council;

22 October, Secretary of State confirms Paradise Project will not be called in;

13 December, city council resolves to use CPOs for land assembly;

19 December, Grosvenor and city council sign development agreement, and Section 106 clauses agreed;

23 December, planning permission issued along with listed buildings consents.

2003

29 January, Liverpool nominated as World Heritage Site;

21 March, city council issues draft compulsory purchase orders (CPOs);

8 April, planning permission granted for removal and rebuild of fire station;

4 June, Liverpool named European Capital of Culture for 2008;

October, John Lewis announces move to new anchor store;

19 December, Laing O'Rourke selected as 'construction partner'.

2004

February, revised planning application submitted;

Spring, detailed design of major works starts. Archaeological investigations and enabling works begin;

2 July, historic parts of Liverpool's dock front listed as World Heritage Site;

17 November, public information centre opens;

22 November, principal building work begins.

2005

13 June, tram project cancelled;

Autumn, main letting campaign starts;

1 November, Paradise Project rebranded as 'Liverpool One';

13 November, new bus station/ticket office opens;

21 November, multi-storey Liver Street car park opens;

25 November, Mike Storey resigns as leader of Liverpool City Council. Replaced by Warren Bradley.

2006

30 January, Sir David Henshaw quits as chief executive of Liverpool City Council, effective from 31 March;

March, Balfour Beatty (and subsidiaries) selected to construct area to east of Paradise Street;

May, first tranche of mid-size retailers signed up to the development announced;

August, John Lewis and new, relocated fire station building completed.

2007

1 February, BBC Radio Merseyside building opens;

February, apartments in One Park West building begin to be sold off-plan;

March, Debenhams and John Lewis take possession of their new stores;

May, Herbert the Hairdresser moves into the 'Bling Bling' building;

August, planting of Chavasse Park begins.

2008

29 May, opening of Phase One of Liverpool One, comprising South John Street, the two anchor stores and Paradise Street;

1 October, Chavasse Park opened by Princess Royal and Duke of Westminster. The entire development site (bar Hilton hotel and One Park West) now open to public.

2009

Spring, completion of Hilton hotel and restoration of properties along School Lane and Hanover Street.

Appendix B
THE TEAM

The complexity of generating and delivering a masterplan for the Paradise Street area was such that a large team of specialist consultants was assembled over a period of four years. Because of the scale of the project, and Grosvenor's determination to create a city centre of variety and character, the development area was subdivided into 34 plots, designed by 26 firms of architects.

FUNDERS

The Grosvenor Liverpool Fund was financed by investors:

Grosvenor

Aberdeen Property Investors (on behalf of a private Middle Eastern Client)

Hermes (on behalf of Britel Fund Trustees and Possfund Custodian Trustees)

Liverpool Victoria

Maroon Capital

Redevco Properties UK

Four banks also provided loans for the project:

Barclays

Eurohypo

HSBC

Royal Bank of Scotland

The arrangement of the funding package was facilitated by DTZ.

CORE MASTERPLANNING TEAM

Grosvenor

Building Design Partnership, masterplanners

Capita Symonds, highways designers and health and safety advisers

Davis Langdon, cost consultants

Drivers Jonas, planning consultants

Liverpool City Council

Nightingale Associates, access consultants

Pelli Clarke Pelli Architects, urban design consultants

Waterman Partnership, structural and environmental engineers

WSP Group, infrastructure and building services engineers

PROPERTY/PLANNING CONSULTANTS

Edmund Kirby

CBRE

Cushman & Wakefield

Keppie Massie

Strutt & Parker

Tushingham Moore

LEGAL TEAMS

Allen & Overy

Berwin Leighton Paisner

Boodle Hatfield

Brabners Chaffe Street

Denton Wilde Sapte

Nabarro

Slaughter and May

CONTRACTORS

Balfour Beatty, east of Paradise Street

Kier, Hilton hotel

Laing O'Rourke, west of Paradise Street

Mansell, Site 8

ARCHITECTS
Aedas
Allies and Morrison
Austin-Smith:Lord
BDP
Brock Carmichael
Craig Foster Architects
CZWG
Dixon Jones Architects
FAT
Glenn Howells Architects
Greig & Stephenson
Gross Max
Groupe Six
Hawkins\Brown
Haworth Tompkins
John McAslan + Partners
Leach Rhodes Walker
Limbrick Architecture
and Design
Marks Barfield Architects
Squire & Partners
Owen Ellis Partnership
Page\Park
Pelli Clarke Pelli Architects
Stephenson Bell Architects
Studio Three
Wilkinson Eyre Architects

ENGINEERS
Arup
FHP
Hoare Lea
Paul Moy Associates
Pell Frischmann
Sheppard Robson

MARKETING
Bostock and Pollitt
Finch Ltd
GMJ
JWT Cheetham Bell
Klein O'Rorke
Mason Williams
MediaVest
Quiller
Sutton Young
Think PR
Wolff Olins

OTHER KEY SUPPLIERS
Acuity Management Solutions
Ltd, facilities management

Broadgate Estates,
property management

Clarus Consulting,
programme management

Cyril Sweett, retail delivery

EC Harris, project management

Emma Robinson Consulting,
asset management

Gardiner & Theobald, surveyor

King Sturge, surveyor

Knight Frank, surveyor

KPMG, tax advisers

Ray Cliff Consulting,
property management

Realty, insurer

Turner & Townsend Cost
Management, quantity surveyor

Watts & Partners, surveyor

Appendix C
THE CONSULTEES

Securing the views and support of a wide range of stakeholders and interested parties was crucial to the successful delivery of Liverpool One. During the eight years from inception to delivery, Grosvenor consulted with:

Ancient Monuments Society

Artists Club

Bluecoat Chambers

Civic Society

Commission for Architecture and the Built Environment

Council for British Archaeology

Courts Service

English Heritage

English Partnerships

Georgian Society

Government Office North West

Hope Street Association

Landowners and occupiers

Liverpool Chamber of Commerce and Industry

Liverpool City Central: BID

Liverpool City Council

Liverpool Fire Service

Liverpool Urban Design and Conservation Advisory Panel

Liverpool Vision

Liverpool Vision Focus Group

Liverpool Waterfront and Commercial Centre

Merseyside Archaelogical Service

Merseyside Civic Society

Merseyside Cycle Campaign

Merseyside Police HQ

Merseyside Police Liaison Service

Merseyside Site and Monuments Board

Merseyside Traffic Police Liaison Service

Merseytravel

Northwest Regional Development Agency

Residents' associations

Rope Walks Partnership

Twentieth Century Society

Urban Design Group (NW)

Victorian Society

Appendix D
KEY FACTS

Although Liverpool One is a retail-led development, it is decidedly a mixed-use scheme incorporating, for example, studio facilities for the BBC, a Quaker Meeting House, homes, a cinema, restaurants, hotels and parkland. The vital statistics of this 42 acre (17 hectare) project include:

TOTAL SPACE
2.5 million square feet (234,000 square metres)

OFFICE SPACE
35,000 square feet (3,250 square metres)

RETAIL
1.4 million square feet (130,000 square metres)

175 retail units

LEISURE
230,000 square feet (21,500 square metres)

RESIDENTIAL
over 500 units

CAR PARKING
3,000 spaces

DEPARTMENT STORE 1 (JOHN LEWIS)
240,000 square feet (22,300 square metres)

DEPARTMENT STORE 2 (DEBENHAMS)
185,000 square feet (17,200 square metres)

HOTEL 1 (HILTON)
270 rooms

HOTEL 2 (ACCOR)
107 rooms

OPEN SPACE
5.5 acres (2.2 hectares)

Appendix E
THE TENANTS

The following lists retailers and restaurants that had either already opened in Liverpool One, or signed an intention to do so, by 1 October 2008.

Accessorize
Adams
Adidas
Aldo
All Saints
American Apparel
Ann Summers
Apple
Austin Reed
Bank Store
Barburrito
Barclays Bank PLC
Barratts
Bathstore
BBC Shop
Bench
Blue Inc
Body Shop
Build-a-Bear Workshop
Café Rouge
Cafe Sports Express
Carphone Warehouse
Chayophraya
Claire's Accessories
Clinton Cards
Costa Coffee
Crocs
Cult
Debenhams
Dirty Kidz
Disney Store

Drome
Dune
Ernest Jones
Esprit
Faith
Fat Face
Flannels
Foot Asylum
Fred Perry
Game
GAP
Goldsmiths
Gourmet Burger Kitchen
Greggs
G Star
Henleys
Henri Lloyd
Herberts
HMV
H & M
H Samuel
Jane Norman
JD
Jigsaw
John Lewis
Jones Bootmaker
Karen Millen
Korova
Lacoste
Lakeland
La Senza

Las Iguanas
Leia Lingerie
Liverpool FC Store
L'Occitane
Lollipops Paris
Mango
Mario's Sandwich Bar
Monsoon
Nandos
NatWest
New Look
Nike
Odeon
Office
Onitsuka Tiger
Optical Express
Orange
O2
Peacocks
Perfume Shop
Pesto
Pizza Hut
Pret A Manger
Principles
Pull and Bear
Puma
Q-Park
Radley
Reiss Ladies
Republic
Script

Shakeabout
Sports Direct
SONY
Starbucks
Suits You
Superdrug
Swarovski
Ted Baker
Thorntons
Topshop/Topman
3 Store
2 Joes Cafe
Urban Outfitters
USC
Vodafone
Wagamama
Warehouse
Watch Workshop
Waterstone's
WH Smith
Yee Rah
Yo Sushi
Zara
Zara Home
Zizzi

Appendix F
BIBLIOGRAPHY

This book was made possible by listening to the private recollections of many individuals close to the Liverpool One project, as well as by being given access to confidential documents held by Grosvenor. The local and property press were also useful, notably the *Liverpool Daily Post*, the *Liverpool Echo*, *Property Week* and the *Estates Gazette*. Documents and publications which proved to be particularly enlightening, many of which are either referred to or quoted in this book, include:

Architectural Review, January 2008

By Design. Urban design in the planning system: towards better practice, Department of Environment, Transport and the Regions/Commission for Architecture and the Built Environment, 2000

Duke Street Bold Street Integrated Action Plan, Liverpool City Council, 1998

Future of Retail Property; shopping places for people, British Council of Shopping Centres, 2007

Grosvenor annual reports, 2006 and 2007

Journal of Retail & Leisure Property, 'Regeneration and retail in Liverpool: a new approach', Charlie Parker and Catherine Garnell, Vol 5, No 4

Landscape, April 2004

Liverpool PSDA Economic Assessment, Drivers Jonas, April 2003

Liverpool Economic Briefing. A monitor of employment and wealth generation (1995–2005/6), Document PMD 371, produced by Regeneration Policy, Programmes & Performance Division, Liverpool City Council

Liverpool One. Rule 7. Think Again, Grosvenor marketing document

National Survey of Local Shopping Patterns, CB Richard Ellis, 2008

Paradise Street Development Area economic assessment, Drivers Jonas, January 2001

Paradise Street Development Area Masterplan Report, submitted by Grosvenor to Liverpool City Council, January 2001. Revised October 2001 and February 2004

Paradise Street Development Area submission by Grosvenor Developments Ltd and Henderson Investors Ltd, August 1999

Proof of Evidence of Michael John Burchnall on Behalf of the City of Liverpool, evidence to public inquiry (on compulsory purchase orders), 2003

Proof of Evidence of Mark A McVicar, Commercial Evidence on Behalf of the City of Liverpool, evidence to public inquiry (on revisions to the UDP), 2001

Proof of Evidence of Peter Drummond on Behalf of the City of Liverpool, evidence to public inquiry (on compulsory purchase orders), 2003

Proof of Evidence of Rodney Holmes on Behalf of the City of Liverpool, evidence to public inquiry (on compulsory purchase orders), 2003

PSDA Development Brief, Healey & Baker, November 2000

Regeneration and Development in Liverpool City Centre 1995–2004, the City of Liverpool and Liverpool Vision, July 2004

Retail Property Review, September 2007

Strategic Regeneration Framework, Liverpool Vision, July 2000

Summary of Proof of Evidence of Mark A McVicar, on Behalf of the City of Liverpool, evidence to public inquiry (on compulsory purchase orders), 2003

Towards a Strong Urban Renaissance. An independent report by members of the Urban Taskforce chaired by Lord Rogers of Riverside, Department of Environment, Transport and the Regions, November 2005

Towards an Urban Renaissance. Final report of the Urban Taskforce chaired by Lord Rogers of Riverside, Department of Environment, Transport and the Regions, June 1999

Unfamiliar Journeys, Alan McKernan, University of Liverpool Press, 2006

Urban Design, Autumn 2005, No 96

What Kind of World Are We Building? The privatisation of public space, Anna Minton, Royal Institute of Chartered Surveyors, 2006

Appendix G
INTERVIEW LIST

The author would like to express his thanks to all the people who gave their time during the research of this book. Those formally interviewed, face-to-face or via the telephone, were:

Bill Allen, Grosvenor,
17 June 2008

Richard Barkham, Grosvenor,
12 and 24 June 2008

Robert Barnes, Dixon Jones
Architects, 12 September 2008

Bill Butler, Pelli Clarke Pelli
Architects, 7 October 2008

Guy Butler, Grosvenor,
17 July 2008

John Bullough, Aldar,
19 September 2008

Giulia Bunting, Drivers
Jonas, 9 July 2008 and
27 August 2008

Michael Burchnall, Liverpool City
Council, 30 September 2008

Julia Chowings, Drivers Jonas,
27 August 2008

Ayo Daramola-Martin,
Grosvenor, 1 October 2008

Terry Davenport, Building Design
Partnership, 30 May 2008 and
1 July 2008

Sir Jeremy Dixon, Dixon Jones
Architects, 12 September 2008

Sarah-Jane Farr, Merseyside
Archaeological Service,
15 October 2008

Jenefer Greenwood, Grosvenor,
26 June 2008

Brian Hatton,
30 September 2008

Hendrik Heyns, Allies
and Morrison Architects,
2 September 2008

Rod Holmes, Grosvenor,
18 June 2008 and 17 July 2008

Mervyn Howard, Grosvenor,
19 November 2008

John Irvine, Grosvenor,
2 October 2008

Margaret Jacques, John Lewis,
18 June 2008

Tim Makower, Allies
and Morrison Architects,
2 September 2008

Richard Mander, Grosvenor,
9 October 2008

John McAslan, John McAslan
+ Partners, 1 October 2008

Stephen Musgrave, Hines,
5 September 2008

Jeremy Newsum, Grosvenor,
26 June 2008

Henry Owen-John, English
Heritage, 26 September 2008

Mark Preston, Grosvenor,
21 November 2008

Trevor Skempton, architectural
consultant, 30 September 2008

John Stonard, CABE,
13 October 2008

Jack Stopforth, Liverpool
Chamber of Commerce,
18 June 2008

Mike Storey, Liverpool City
Council, 1 July 2008

Gareth Thomas, John Lewis,
9 July 2008

Peter Vernon, Grosvenor,
25 November 2008

This book has also been
informed by countless
informal conversations with
people involved with Liverpool
One, including architects,
consultants, policy makers
and other industry insiders.
Thanks to them all.

Appendix H
GROSVENOR STAFF DIRECTLY INVOLVED IN LIVERPOOL ONE

James Alderson
Bill Allen
Claire Barber
Neil Barber
Nicola Bareham
Richard Barkham
Nicola Beausire
Lucy Bennett
Chris Bliss
Sharon Bloodworth
Steve Brewer
Jenny Brown
Kate Brown
John Bullough
Will Burr
Guy Butler
Simon Camp
Laurence Chadwick
Suat Cheung
Yee Chong
Fiona Clare
Alison Clegg
Nick Constable
Naomi Currey
Mark Curry
Sarah-Jane Curtis
Ayo Daramola-Martin
Lorraine Dolding
Corinne Dourado
Cindy Downing
Miles Dunnett
Mark Ellison
Angela Farr
Richard Fawcus

Hunter Finlayson
Linda Forth
Richard Fowke
Helen Freeman
Steven Garrett
John German
Rachel Good
Iain Greenwood
Jenefer Greenwood
Jonathan Hagger
Richard Handley
Alex Henderson
Elaine Hicks
Phil Hobson
Lucy Hodder
Rodney Holmes
Stephen Horner
Mervyn Howard
John Irvine
Joanne Jennings
Chris Jukes
Derek Kay
Richard Keen
Liam Kelly
Bhupen Kerai
Kate Kilborn
Hilary Kinsella
Roz Langford
Christopher Lee
Clare Leyden
Richard Mallett
Richard Mander
Beatrice McEvoy
Susan Moore

Stephen Musgrave
Jeremy Newsum
Mike Nisbet
Jayne Onslow
David Parsons
Rory Penn
Tina Pickles
Mark Preston
Carol Randall
Philip Riley
Sheila Roberts
Emma Robinson
Katie Robinson
Rachel Scott
Susan Shaw
Edward Skeates
Lauren Smith
Caroline Smithson
Justin St Clair Charles
James Stevens
Dan Symonds
Chris Taite
Heather Thompson
Tom Uttley
John Venters
Peter Vernon
Rachel Wadsworth
Ed Webb
Ann Wheat
Janet Whiting
Sarah Wright
Rachel Wright

INDEX

PICTURE CREDITS